SAMSUNG GALAXY S22 USER GUIDE FOR SENIORS

The Illustrated Manual for Samsung Galaxy S22, S22+, and S22 Ultra

Joseph F. Morris

Copyright © 2022 by Joseph F. Morris

All rights reserved.

No part of this book may be reproduced, distributed, or transmitted in any form, or by any means, including recording, photocopying, or other mechanical or electronic methods, without the prior written permission of the publisher, except in the case of brief quotations embodied in critical reviews and certain other non-commercial uses permitted by copyright laws.

Table of Content

Introduction 19
Chapter 1: Getting Started 21
Install SIM Card 21
Set Up Your Device 22
Hardware Buttons 23
Wireless Power Sharing 24
Transfer Data from An Old Device 26
Transfer Your Data Using a USB Cable 26
Transfer Data with Wi-Fi Direct 28
Transfer Backed Up Data from Your PC 28
Access Settings App 29
Search for Settings 29
Set the Side Key 30
Activate an eSIM 30
Manage SIM Settings 31
Turn Device On 32
Turn Device Off 32
Restart Device 32
Use Side Key to Power Off Device 33
Force Restart the Samsung S22 33
Emergency Mode 34

Chapter 2: Notification Panel 35
Open and Close the Notification Panel 35
Functions on the Notification Panel 36
Control Nearby Devices 38
Control Media Playback 38
Quick Setting Options 39

Chapter 3: The Navigation Bar 40
Use Navigation Gestures 41

Chapter 4: Motion and Gestures 43
Alert When Picked Up 43
Lift to Wake 43
Keep Screen Off While Viewing 44
Double Tap to Turn Screen On or Off 45
Mute with Gestures 45

Chapter 5: Language and Input 47
Change Device Language 47
Change Default Keyboard 47
Device Date and Time 48
Password and Autofill 48
Customization Service 49

Chapter 6: Home and App Screens 50
Switch Between App and Home Screens 50

Add Apps Button on the Home Screen 51
Customize the Home Screen 51
Set Wallpaper.. 52
Edit Home Screen Panels 54
Samsung's Finder 55
Add App Shortcut to Home Screen 56
Create, Delete and Move App Folders.............. 56
Show All Apps on the Home Screen 57
App Screen Grid... 58
Home Screen Grid 58
Folder Grid... 59
Add Media Page to HOME screen 59
Lock Home Screen Layout............................... 60
Add New Apps to Home Screen 60
Hide Apps 60
Swipe Down for Notification Panel 61
Rotate to Landscape Mode 61

Chapter 7: Using Apps 63
Uninstall or Disable Apps................................ 63
Find Apps... 63
Sort Apps... 64
Choose Default Apps 64

Game Booster 65

Samsung App Settings 65

Chapter 8: Screen Record and Screen Capture 66

Screen Record 66

Change Screen Recorder Settings 67

Capture a Screenshot 67

Turn on the Screenshot Toolbar 69

Screenshot Settings 69

Chapter 9: Edge Panel 71

Turn on Edge Panel 71

Apps Panel 72

Configure Apps Panel 72

Configure Edge Panels 73

Edge Panel Position and Style 74

Chapter 10: Galaxy S22 Ultra S Pen 76

Store and Detach the S Pen 76

Charge the S Pen 77

Reset Your S Pen 77

Air Actions 78

Hold the S Pen Button Shortcut 79

Anywhere Actions 80

App Actions 81
Take Pictures with the S Pen 81
General App Actions 82
Air Command..83
Air Command Icon 84
Turn on the Air Command Icon 85
Smart Select 85
Capture Parts of a Video 86
Screen Write 88
Live Messages 89
Translate 90
Glance 92
Write on Calendar..93
S Pen to Text 94
Air View...94
Pen Select 95
Screen Off Memo 95
Pin a Screen Off Memo on the Always on Display
....96
Unlock Your Screen with the S Pen...................97
Show Pointer When Hovering............................98
Allow Multiple S Pen 98

Keep S Pen Connected 98

The Appearance of the Air Command 99

Shortcut Settings 99

Open Air command with Pen Button 99

Warn if S Pen is Left Behind 100

When S Pen is Removed 100

S Pen Sound Customization 100

Chapter 11: Biometric Security 102

Face Recognition 102

Delete Face Data 102

Add Alternative Appearance 102

Face Unlock 103

Stay on Lock Screen Until Swipe 103

Other Face Recognition Management 104

Fingerprint Scanner 104

Add, Delete and Rename Fingerprints 105

Fingerprint Verification Settings 106

Biometric Settings 107

Security Update 108

Private Share 108

Turn on Find My Mobile 109

Secure Folder 110

Secure Folder Settings 111

Access Secure Folder 111

Set Up SIM Card Lock 112

Install Unknown Apps 113

View Passwords 113

Pin Windows 113

Chapter 12: Contacts App..................... 116

Create New Contact 116

Import Contact 116

Sync Contacts with Your Web Accounts 117

Edit a Contact 117

Favorites 118

Search for Contacts 118

Share Contacts 119

Delete Contacts 119

Show Contacts when Sharing Content 119

Create Groups 120

Add or Remove Group Contacts 120

Send a Message to a Group 121

Merge Duplicate Contacts 121

Delete a Group 122

Emergency Contacts 122

Chapter 13: Phone App 123
Make Calls on S22 123
Call from Your Contact List or Call Logs 124
Set Speed Dial 124
Remove a Number from Speed Dial 125
Make International Calls 125
Answer a Call 126
Reject a Call 126
Make a Multi-Party Call 126
Video Call Effects 127
Block Phone Numbers 127
Wi-Fi Calling 128

Chapter 14: Messages App 129
Send New Message 129
View Messages 130
Sort Messages 130
Delete Conversations 131
Send SOS Messages 131
Change Message Settings 133

Chapter 15: Calendar App 134
Add Accounts to Calendar App 134
Calendar Alert Style 135

Create an Event 136

Delete an Event 136

Chapter 16: Internet 137

Access the Browser 137

Browser Tabs 138

Create Bookmark 138

Open a Bookmark 138

Save a Webpage 139

Share Webpages... 139

View/ Clear Browsing History......................... 139

Browse on Secret Mode 140

Secret Mode Settings 140

Chapter 17: Camera App 142

Navigate the Camera Screen........................... 142

Space Zoom.. 143

Set Shooting Mode... 143

Record Videos 145

Zoom-in Mic 145

Scene Optimization.. 146

Shot Suggestions.. 146

Scan QR Codes 147

Swipe Shutter Button..147

Selfie Settings 148

Choose Picture Formats 148

Video Settings 149

Advanced Video Recording Options 149

General Camera Setting.................................. 150

Shooting Methods... 151

Camera Settings to Keep................................. 153

Chapter 18: Clock App 154

Set Alarms 154

Set Your Sleep and Wake Time 155

Delete an Alarm 156

Alert Settings 156

World Clock 156

Time Zone Converter 158

Weather Settings.. 158

Stopwatch 159

Preset Time 159

Timer Options 160

Chapter 19: Gallery App........................ 161

View Pictures 161

Edit Photos.. 163

Play Video 164

Video Brightness 164
Edit Video 165
Share Videos and Pictures 166
Delete Media Contents 166
Group Similar Images 166

Chapter 20: My Files 167
File Groups 167
Trash Folder 168
Delete Items from My File 169
Large File Size Settings 169

Chapter 21: Samsung Pay 171
Set Up Samsung Pay 171
Use Samsung Pay 173
Quick Access 173

Chapter 22: Samsung Notes 175
Create New Notes 175
Voice Recordings 176
Edit Notes 176
Open PDFs in Samsung Note 176
Search Notes 177
Sort Notes 177
Delete, Share, Move Notes 177

Change Page View 177
View Trash Folder 178

Chapter 23: Accounts 179
Add a Google Account 179
Add a Samsung Account 179
Add an Outlook Account 180
Account Settings 180
Remove an Account 180

Chapter 24: Connections 182
Connect to a Wi-Fi Network 182
Manage Saved Networks 182
Advanced Wi-Fi Settings 182
Connect to Bluetooth 185
Rename Paired Bluetooth Device 186
Unpair From a Bluetooth Device 186
Change your Phone's Bluetooth Name 186
Advanced Options 187
Bluetooth Control History 187
Bluetooth Scan History 188
Airplane Mode 188
Mobile Networks 189
Check Data Usage 189

Turn on Data Saver 189

Mobile Hotspot 190

Auto Hotspot 190

Nearby Device Scanning 191

Connect to a Printer 191

Chapter 25: Notification 192

Notification Pop-Up Style 192

Recently Sent Notifications 193

Do Not Disturb 194

Hide Notifications 195

Show Notification Icons 196

Show Battery Percentage 196

View Notification History 196

Floating Notifications 197

Notification Reminders 197

Advanced Notification Settings 198

Chapter 26: Sounds and Vibrations 200

Sound Mode 200

Vibration 201

Device Volume 201

Media Volume Limit 202

Ringtone 203

Notification Sound 203

System Sounds 203

Dolby Atmos 204

Equalizer 204

UHQ Upscaler 205

Adapt Sound 205

Separate App Sound 206

Chapter 27: Display 208

Easy Mode 208

Show Charging Information 208

Dark Mode 209

Screen Brightness 210

Motion Smoothness 211

Eye Comfort Shield 211

Screen Mode 212

Screen Resolution 213

Font Style and Size 213

Screen Zoom 214

Full-Screen Apps 215

Screen Timeout 215

Accidental Touch Protection 216

Touch Sensitivity 216

Screen Saver 216

One-Handed Mode 217

Chapter 28: Lock Screen and Security ... 219

Set a Secure Screen Lock 219

Change Lock Screen Method 221

Factory Data Reset for Lock Screen 221

Smart Lock 222

Screen Lock Settings..222

Chapter 29: Always on Display 224

Turn on Always on Display..............................224

Show Music Information on AOD 224

AOD Clock Style 225

AOD Auto-Brightness 226

AOD Themes 227

Chapter 30: Mobile Continuity 228

Link to Window 228

Samsung DeX...229

Continue Apps on Other Devices 229

Multi-Window..230

Window Controls 231

Chapter 31: Location Services.................232

Turn on Location Services 232

App Permissions 232

Recent Access 232

Emergency Location Service 233

Chapter 32: Device Maintenance 234

Quick Optimization 234

Set Up Quick Charging 234

Set Power Sharing Limit 235

Tips to Save Battery Power 236

View Battery Usage Since Last Full Charge 236

Battery Power Saving 237

Battery Background Usage Limit 237

Adaptive Battery 237

Protect Battery 238

Manage Storage 238

Manage Memory 239

Advanced Device Care Options 239

Chapter 33: Troubleshooting 241

System/ Software Updates 241

Reset all Phone Settings 242

Reset Network Setting 242

Reset Accessibility Settings 242

Auto-Restart Device 243

Factory Data Reset..243

Remove Secure Lock Screen............................244

Chapter 34: Digital Wellbeing and Parental Controls 245

View Dashboard...245

Set Screen Time Goal...245

App Timers 246

Focus Mode..246

Bedtime Mode..247

Volume Monitor...248

Driving Monitor...248

Parental Control 249

Chapter 35: Other Settings 250

Android Auto 250

Dual Messenger 251

Smart Suggestions 251

Medical Info...252

Quick Share..252

Samsung Labs 254

About Phone 254

Conclusion 255

Introduction

The Samsung Galaxy S22, S22+, and S22 Ultra are the latest flagship phones from the Samsung brand. Unlike the previous models, the Samsung Galaxy S22 Ultra comes with the S Pen that you can use to operate your device seamlessly. Samsung says that the S22 S Pen is 70% more responsive than the one designed for the S21 Ultra, therefore making you feel like you are using a real pen to write or doodle.

The trio has ultrasonic fingerprint sensors to secure your device. They are all IP68 water/ dust resistance, protecting the phone from damage from a liquid. Their screens are also made of Gorilla Glass Victus Plus, the strongest glass found on any phone.

The three phones ship with the Android 12, Android's latest operating software that comes with several features you can maximize to get out more from your smartphone.

Whether you have the S22, S22+, or S22 Ultra, this user guide has compiled all the amazing features and provided step-by-step instructions on how you can master these features and get the best out of your latest smartphone.

Chapter 1: Getting Started

Find all the settings you need to prepare your phone for use.

Install SIM Card

The S22 allows you to use a physical SIM card and an eSIM. An eSIM is a digital SIM that your service provider will give you when requested. Note that the eSIM service is not available for all regions and countries. Follow the steps below to insert the physical SIM

- Open the SIM card tray using the ejection pin that is included in the phone pack
- Draw out the tray and place your SIM in the allocated space.
- Press the SIM gently to ensure it is well fitted, then push the tray back into place.

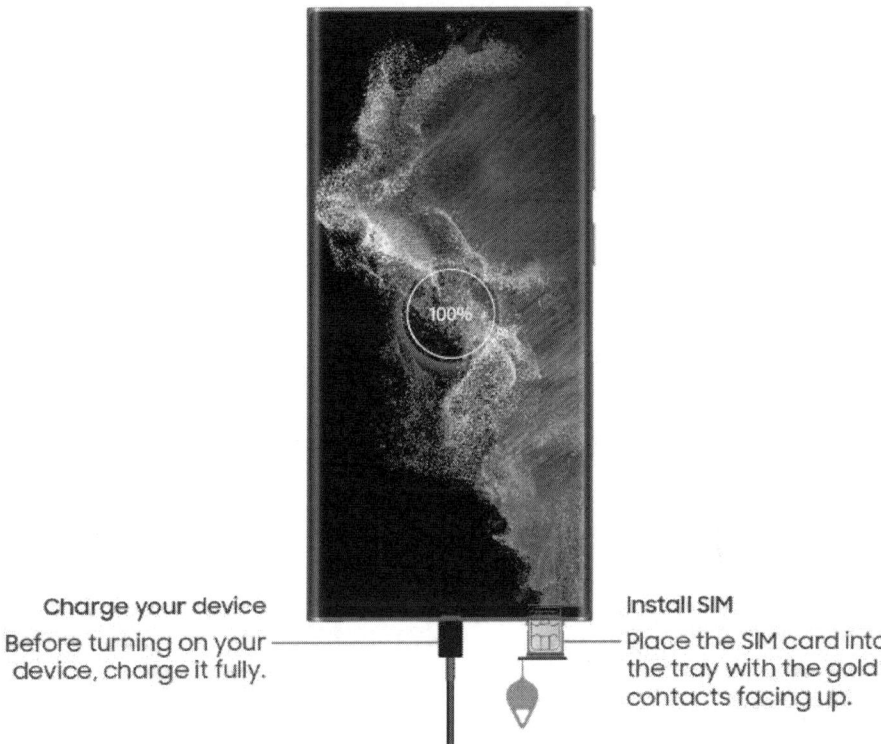

Charge your device
Before turning on your device, charge it fully.

Install SIM
Place the SIM card into the tray with the gold contacts facing up.

Set Up Your Device

When you turn on your phone for the first time, you will find Samsung's setup wizard to guide you through setting up your phone.

- To turn on your phone, press the Side key and hold for some seconds until the screen lights up.
- Choose your language and press the arrow to continue.

- Then follow the on-screen prompts to finish setting up.

Hardware Buttons
Samsung Galaxy S22 and S22+

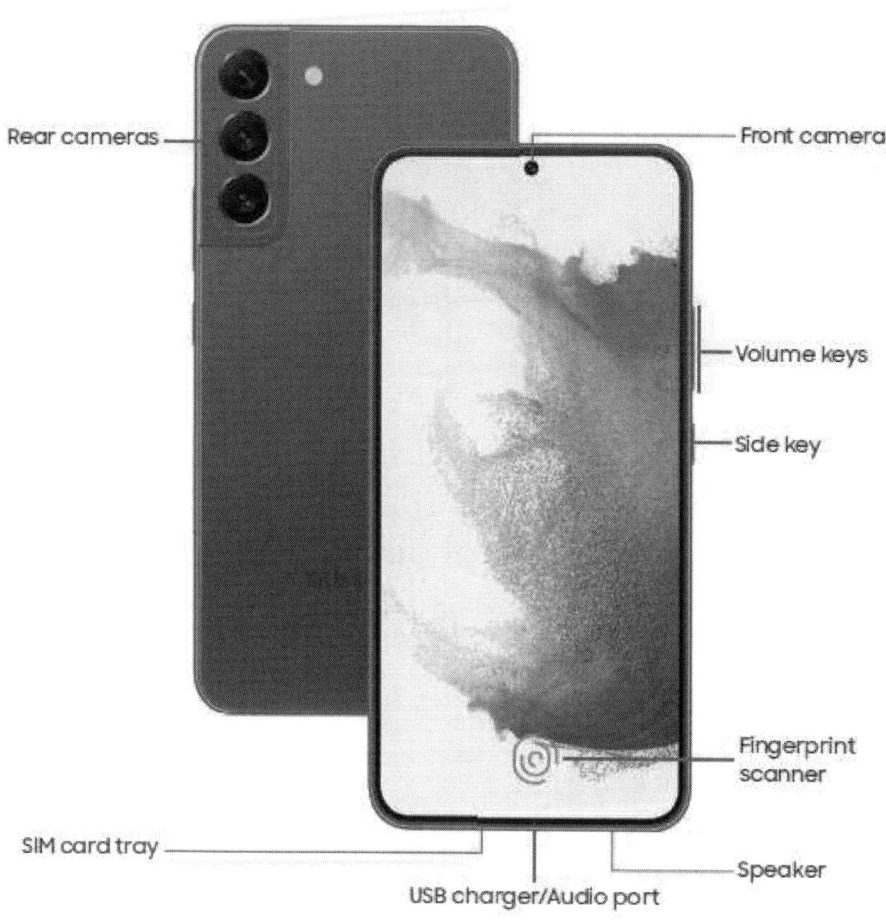

Samsung Galaxy S22 Ultra

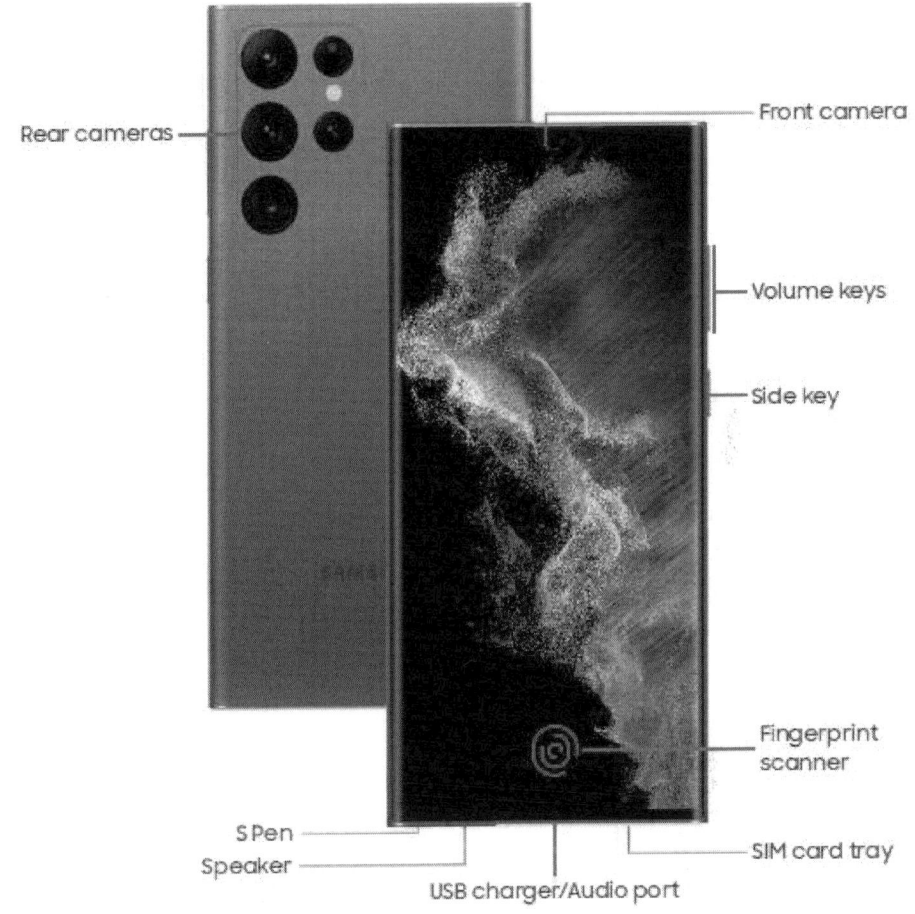

Wireless Power Sharing

With this option, you can use your S22 to charge another device even while charging your S22. For optimized result, it is recommended that you discard any phone cover and accessories before using this option. To use wireless power-sharing,

- Swipe down from the topmost part of any screen to open the 'Notification Panel,' then swipe down again to reveal the quick settings.
- Click the ◉ **Wireless Power Sharing** icon to turn it on. If the ◉ icon isn't showing in the quick setting panel, click ⊕ and drag the ◉ icon into the quick panel.
- Now place the back of the second device on the back of the S22 to begin charging.

Smartphone   Galaxy Watch   Galaxy Buds

- Separate both devices to turn off this setting.

Note: avoid using earphones while wirelessing sharing power as it may affect your nearby devices. You may be unable to access some features on your phone while using this feature. Samsung recommends not using either of the devices while charging.

Transfer Data from An Old Device

With Smart Switch on your S22, you can move data from a previous gadget to your S22. To do this,

- Go to the Settings app and click **Accounts and Backup.**
- Click **Bring Data from Old Device** to continue.

Transfer Your Data Using a USB Cable

One option is to wirelessly transfer data from a previous device. The other option is to connect both devices using a USB cable. Note that you will need to download Smart Switch on both devices.

- Use a compatible USB device to connect the S22 with the old device.

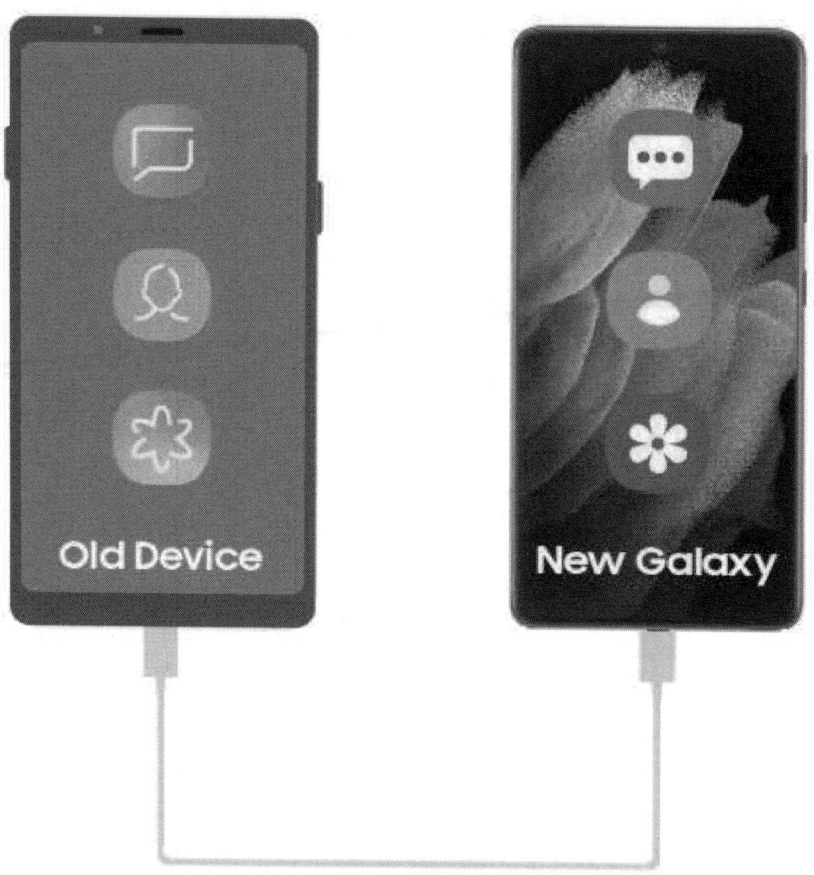

- Click **Smart Switch** on the pop-up window
- Pick the previous device and click **Allow.**
- Choose an option on the S22 and click **Next.**
- Then continue with the guide on your screen.
- You need to keep both devices connected throughout the transfer period.

Transfer Data with Wi-Fi Direct

This is the third way to move data from an old device to the S22.

- Open **Smart Switch** on the old device.
- Unlock the S22, go to the Settings app, click **Accounts and Backup,** then choose the **"Bring Data from Old Device"** option.
- Place both devices close to each other.
- Click **Send data** on the old device and select **Wireless.**
- Click **Receive data** on the S22, choose the operating system for the old device, and select **Wireless.**
- Click **Allow** on your old device.
- Select desired options on the S22, click **Next** to continue.

Transfer Backed Up Data from Your PC

Download the Smart Switch app from the Samsung website, then use the steps below to move backups stored on your computer to your S22:

- Open the Smart Switch app on your computer, then connect the S22 to your computer using a USB Cable.
- Then follow the prompts on your screen to move data from the computer to the S22.

Access Settings App

You will need to go into Settings to change features on your phone. You can access settings in two ways:

- Swipe down from the home screen and click ⚙.
- Go to the App screen and click ⊙ **Settings**

Search for Settings

A quick way to find a setting on your phone is to search for it.

- Open Settings, click 🔍 and enter your keywords.
- Select an item to go right to that setting.

Set the Side Key
The side key (the lower key by the right side of your device) grants you fast access to a feature or an app on your device. To set it up,

- Go to the Settings app and click **Advanced Features.**
- Select **Side Key,** then assign a feature or an app to the side key functions.
- Press & hold the Side Key or press the key twice to access the feature or app.

Activate an eSIM
Follow the options below to set up and begin using an eSIM

- Go to the Settings app and click **Connections.**
- Choose **SIM Card Manager** and select '+' **Add Mobile Plan.'**

- The phone will search for a mobile plan. Once found, use the instructions on the screen to enable the eSIM.

Follow the steps below to activate an eSIM using a QR code from your service provider

- Go to the Settings app and click **Connections.**
- Choose **SIM Card Manager** and select '+' **Add Mobile Plan.'**
- Then select **Scan Carrier QR code** to use the QR code you have

Manage SIM Settings
- Go to the Settings app and click **Connections.**
- Then click on **SIM Card Manager** to customize the following:
    - ➢ **eSIMs:** click to begin using an eSIM
    - ➢ **SIM cards:** use this option to activate your card and change SIM card settings

> **Preferred SIM Card:** assign features and actions to specific SIM cards if using two cards

> **More SIM Card Settings:** access and customize settings for calls and eSIM

Turn Device On
- Press the Side key and hold for some seconds until the screen lights up.

Turn Device Off
- Press and hold the 'Volume Down' key and the Side key simultaneously or Swipe down from the topmost part of your screen to go to the notification panel, then swipe down again and press ⏻.
- Now select **Power Off**

Restart Device
- Press and hold the 'Volume Down' key and the Side key simultaneously or Swipe down from the topmost part of your screen to go to the

notification panel, then swipe down again and press ⏻.

- Then press **Restart**

Use Side Key to Power Off Device
You can set the side key for turning off the device.

- Go to the Settings app and click **Advanced Features.**
- Select **Side Key,** scroll to the **Press and Hold** option and select **Power Off Menu.**
- Now press & hold the Side Key or press the key twice to switch off the device.

Force Restart the Samsung S22
You will need to force restart the device if it suddenly freezes or becomes unresponsive

- Press and hold the 'Volume Down' key and the Side key simultaneously for at least 8 seconds until the screen goes off and comes on again.

Emergency Mode

This mode reduces battery consumption. It comes in handy when you have a low battery level. While it restricts some functions and apps, it still allows you to share your current location with others, make emergency calls, sound an emergency alarm, and lots more. To turn it on,

- Press and hold the 'Volume Down' key and the Side key simultaneously.
- Then select **Emergency Mode.**

To turn it off,

- Press ⋮ and choose "**Turn Off Emergency Mode.**"

Chapter 2: Notification Panel

You will find icons at the top of your screen whenever you have new notifications. Visit the notification panel for more details.

Open and Close the Notification Panel

- Swipe down from the topmost part of your screen to go to the notification panel and swipe up or tap ‹ to exit the panel.
- Click a notification to option it.

- Drag a notification to the right or left to clear it.
- Press **Clear** to delete all notifications
- Press **Notification Settings** to quickly customize notifications

Functions on the Notification Panel

See below some of the functions you can access on the notification panel:

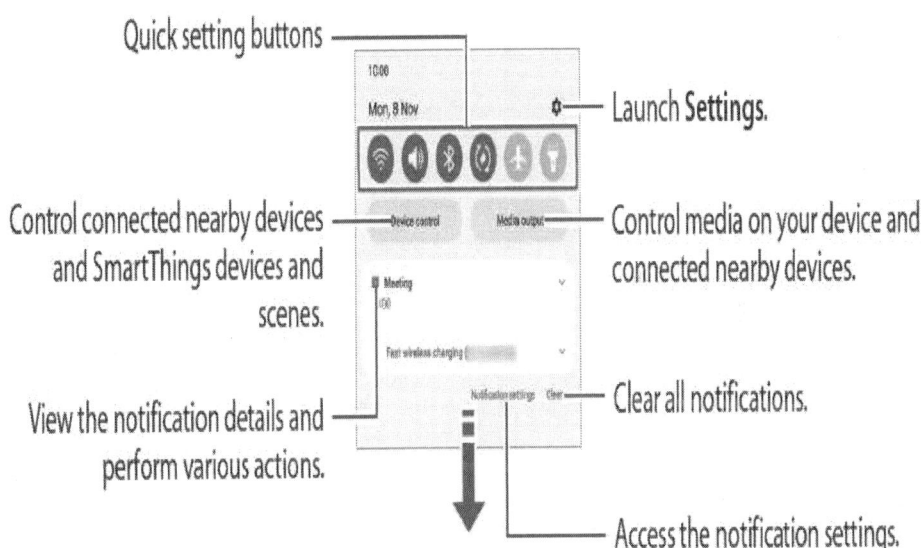

Quick Setting Buttons

Use the quick setting to turn on specific features like Wi-Fi, Bluetooth, and more.

- Swipe down on the notification panel to reveal the quick setting buttons.
- Click a button on the screen to turn it off or on.
- Swipe to the last page of the panel and press ⊕ to add more buttons or features.
- To customize the settings of any of the buttons on this screen, click the text under that button. Click and hold a button to see more settings for that button.

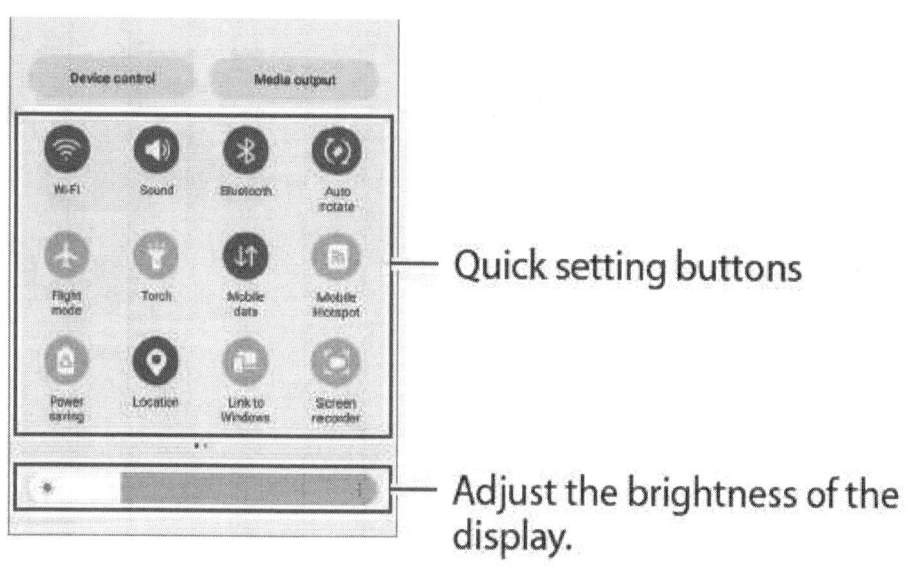

- To move the buttons around, click ⋮, select **Edit Buttons,** then press firmly on a button to highlight it and move it to a different space.

Control Nearby Devices
Control nearby devices right on your S22.

- Swipe down from the topmost part of your screen to go to the notification panel and click **Device Control** to see a list of all nearby SmartThings devices and connected device.
- Choose the device you want to control or click a SmartThings scene to launch it.

Control Media Playback
The media feature on the notification panel is one quick way to control your video or music playback.

- Swipe down from the topmost part of your screen to go to the notification panel and click **Media Output.**
- Use the controller icons to control the media playback.

Quick Setting Options

Here are other options available in the quick setting panel

- Tap 🔍 to use Samsung Finder to search for apps, settings, and other content on your phone.
- Tap ⏻ to access the Restart, Power off, and Emergency mode options.
- Use the slider at the bottom of the screen to modify the screen brightness.

Chapter 3: The Navigation Bar

You can navigate your device using full-screen gestures or the navigation button. The navigation button is easier for most people. You can use the buttons to go Back, go to the home screen, or access Recent apps.

Button		Function
|||	Recents	• Tap to open the list of recent apps.
O	Home	• Tap to return to the Home screen. • Tap and hold to launch the **Google Assistant** app.
<	Back	• Tap to return to the previous screen.

Use Navigation Buttons

Follow the steps below to turn on the navigation button if it is not activated on your device

- Open **Settings,** click **Display,** and select **Navigation Bar.**
- Click **Buttons,** scroll to **Button Order** and choose an arrangement of your choice.

Use Navigation Gestures

Your screen becomes wider when you hide the navigation bar and use swipes in its place. This also means that you would need to master the swipe gestures to perform the functions of the navigation bar.

- Go to the Settings app and click **Display.**
- Click **Navigation Bar** and select **Swipe Gestures.**
- This will automatically hide the Navigation button. However, you will find gesture hints on your screen.

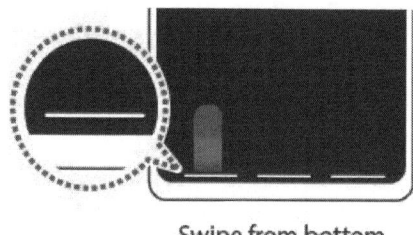
Swipe from bottom

Swipe from sides and bottom

- Switch off the **Gesture Hint** button to turn off the gesture hints after you have mastered using swipe gestures.

- Click **More Options** to select gesture type and sensitivity.

- Turn on **Show Button to Hide Keyboard** to find an icon on the right end side of your device screen to hide the keyboard when using the phone in portrait mode.

- Turn on **Block Gestures with S Pen** (For S22 Ultra only) to block the S Pen from performing navigation gestures.

Chapter 4: Motion and Gestures

Alert When Picked Up

When you pick your phone up, your device can vibrate to let you know you have missed messages and calls. To turn on,

- Open **Settings,** click **Advanced Features.**
- Select **Motions and Gestures** and turn on **Alert When Phone Picked Up.**

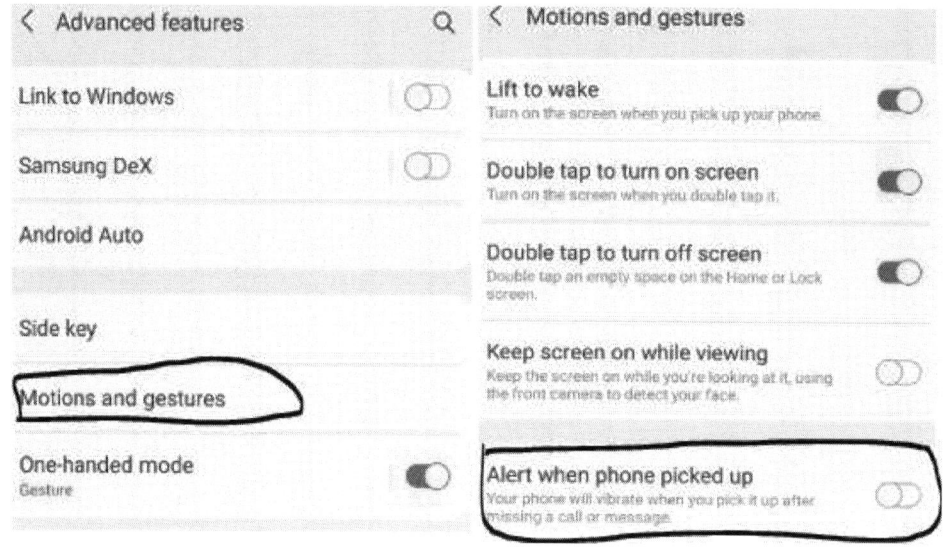

Lift to Wake

Your phone screen will awake once you pick up the device

- Open **Settings,** click **Advanced Features.**
- Select **Motions and Gestures** and turn on **Lift to Wake.**

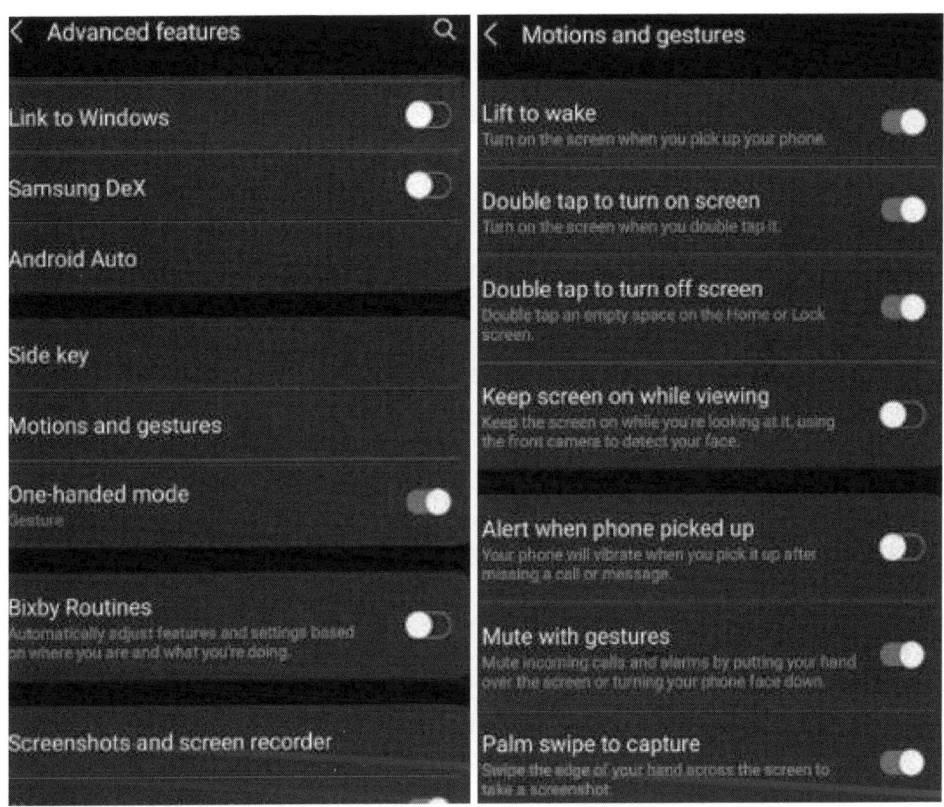

Keep Screen Off While Viewing

The phone goes to sleep if it doesn't feel any tap or touch. However, you can keep it awake as long as you stare into the screen

- Open **Settings,** click **Advanced Features.**

- Select **Motions and Gestures** and turn on **Keep Screen Off While Viewing.**

Double Tap to Turn Screen On or Off
Tap your screen twice to turn it on or off.

- Open **Settings,** click **Advanced Features** & select **Motions and Gestures**
- Then turn on **Double Tap to Turn on Screen** and **Double Tap to Turn off Screen**

Mute with Gestures
Cover your phone with your palm or turn the phone over to mute sounds. To turn on the settings,

- Open **Settings** and click **Advanced Features.**
- Tap **Motion and Gestures,** click **Mute with Gesture,** and turn on the option.

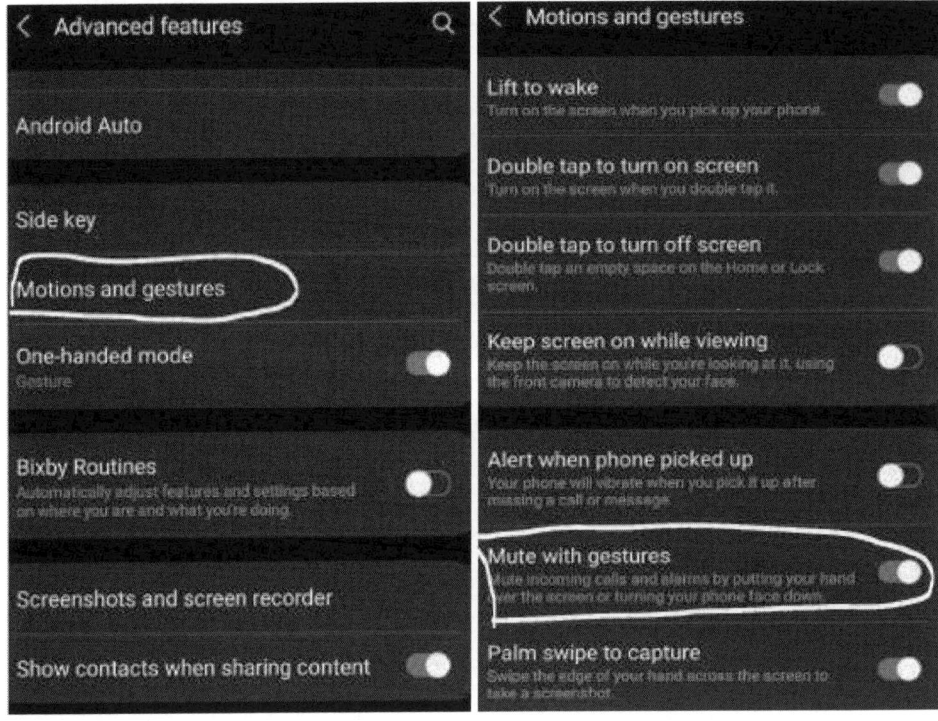

Chapter 5: Language and Input

Choose your desired language and configure input settings

Change Device Language

During setup, you will have the opportunity to choose a language. To change to a different language,

- Open **Settings** and click **General Management.**
- Click **Language** and tap ➕**Add Language.**
- Choose a language and select **Set as Default** to switch to the language.

Change Default Keyboard

Switch to a different keyboard and modify keyboard settings.

- Open **Settings** and click **General Management.**
- Click **Keyboard List and Default,** then click on each option to modify the settings.

Device Date and Time

Your device date and time are set automatically using data from the wireless network. To manually choose the date and time,

- Open **Settings** and click **General Management.**
- Click **Date and Time** for the options below:
    - Turn on '**Automatic Time and Date**' to use the data provided by your network. Disable this option, and you will find the option to **Select Time Zone, Set Date,** and **Set Time.**
    - Turn on '**Set Time Zone Based on Location**' to use your location time zone.
    - Turn on '**Use 24-Hour Format**' to set how you want to view the time.

Password and Autofill

Save your password on your device so that you won't have to manually type it in every time.

- Open **Settings** and click **General Management.**

- Click **Passwords and Autofill** and select an option under **Autofill Service** to choose a medium for saving your passwords.

Customization Service

Samsung can provide you with personalized content after it has reviewed your phone activities. It studies you to know your needs and then suggests content to address the needs. To turn on,

- Open **Settings** and click **General Management.**

- Click **Customization Service** and turn on the feature for desired apps.

Chapter 6: Home and App Screens

The Home screen shows app shortcuts, widgets, and more while the App screen contains all your apps.

Switch Between App and Home Screens

Follow the steps below to move from the home screen to the app screen and back.

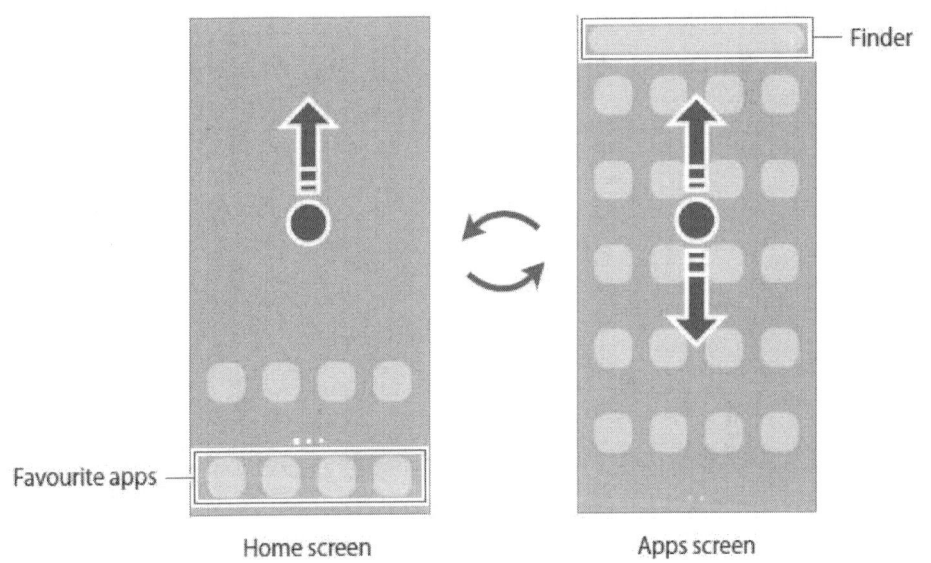

Home screen   Apps screen

- Swipe upwards on the home screen to launch the App Screens.
- Then swipe downwards or upwards on the App screen to return Home. You can also press

50

the home button on the navigation bar to return Home.

Add Apps Button on the Home Screen
No need to swipe up if you have the apps button added to the home screen.

- Tap and hold any empty space on the home screen until you see the settings option.

- Click **Settings** and toggle on the "**Show Apps Screen Button on Home screen**" button.

Customize the Home Screen
Add widgets, choose wallpaper and more for the home screen.

- Tap and hold any empty space on the home screen until you see the settings option.

- Click **Widgets** to add new widgets, choose **Wallpaper and Style** to set new wallpapers or click **Themes** to choose a theme for your device.

Set Wallpaper
Choose a photo or a preloaded wallpaper

- Tap and hold any empty space on the home screen until you see the settings option.
- Choose **Wallpaper and Style** and then choose an option on your screen.
  - ➤ Click **My Wallpapers** to use preloaded wallpapers.
  - ➤ Choose **Gallery** to use a picture or video on your device as your wallpaper.
  - ➤ Click **Lock Screen Wallpaper Services** to use different wallpapers on your lock screen.
  - ➤ Click **Color Palette** to choose a color that matches your wallpaper.
  - ➤ Turn on **Apply Dark Mode to Wallpaper** to change the color of your wallpaper whenever dark mode is on.

- After you select an option above, select a picture or video to continue, choose to have the wallpaper on **Home Screen, Lock Screen,** or both screens.

- Click **Set on Lock/Home Screen** or **Set on Lock and Home Screens.**

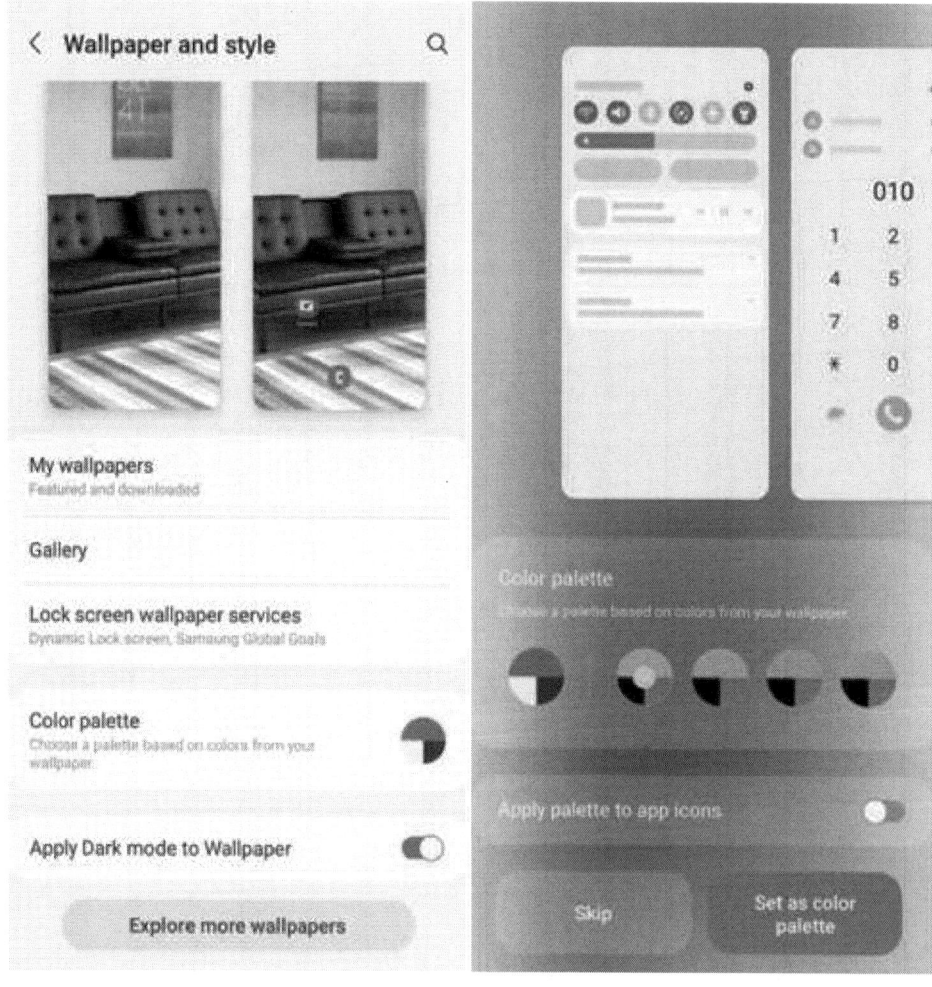

- The screen will automatically suggest colors to go with the background. Click **Set as Color Pallete** or **Skip** to ignore.

Edit Home Screen Panels

Panels are the different screens on the home screen that shows the apps shortcuts and widgets. You can add, remove, or delete a panel with the steps below:

- Tap and hold any empty space on the home screen until you see the settings option.
- Swipe right/ left to the end and click the ⊕ icon to add a new panel
- To rearrange the panels, hold down on a panel to highlight it, then move it to a different location.

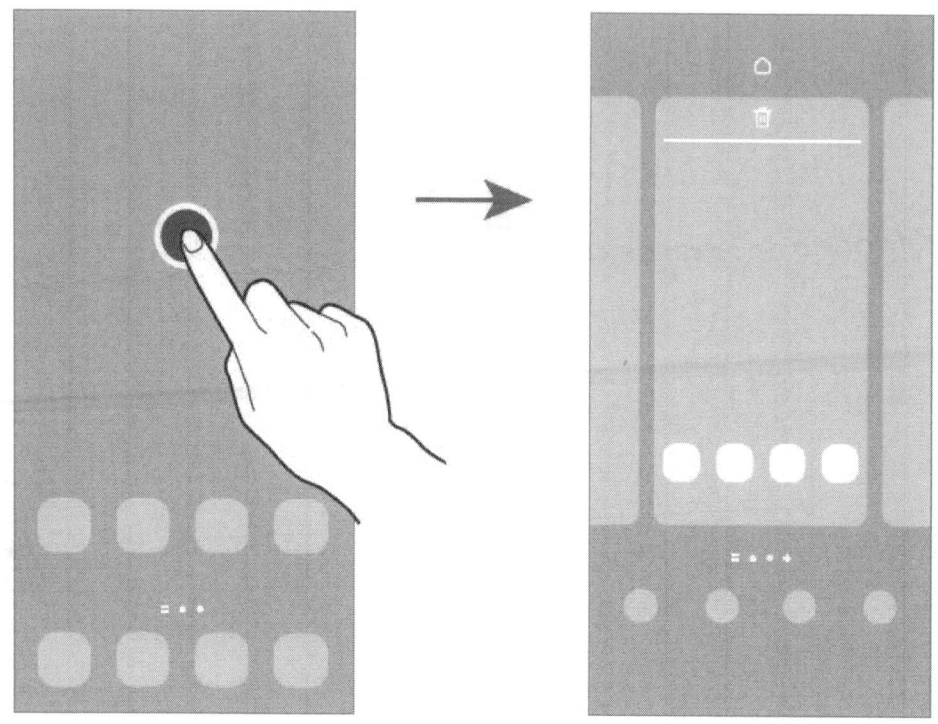

- Tap 🗑 on a panel to delete it.

Samsung's Finder
Use this feature to quickly find content on your S22.

- Swipe up from the home screen to go to the Apps Screen & click **Search.** Or Swipe down from the topmost part of your screen to go to the notification panel, then swipe down again and press 🔍.

- Enter your search phrase to see suggested answers.
- Tap 🔍on your keyboard to view more answers.

Add App Shortcut to Home Screen
Add frequently used apps to your home screen.

- Click and hold the desired app icon on the Apps screen and select the "⊕ **Add to Home**" option.
- You will find the app shortcut on your home screen.

Create, Delete and Move App Folders
Group similar apps into a single folder for quick access.

- Click one app in the Apps or Home screen and drag the app over another to automatically create a new folder.
- Click **Folder Name** to title the new folder.

- To add other apps into the folder, open the folder and click ✛. Select all the desired apps and tap **Done.** Alternatively, drag the new apps and drop them into the folder.

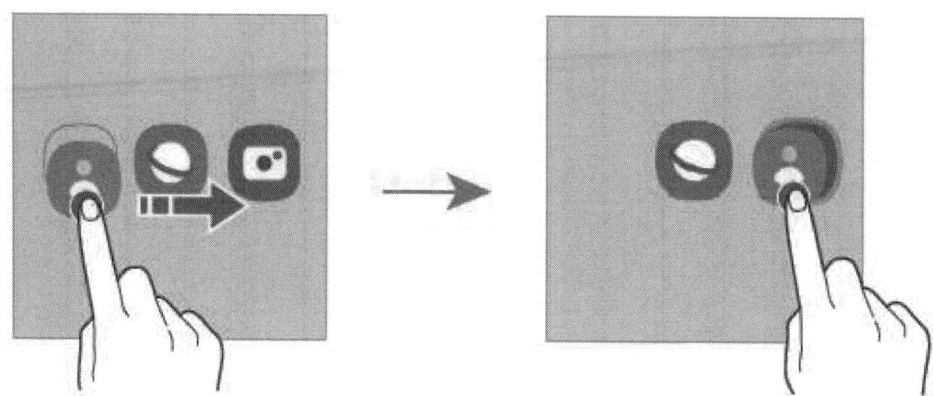

- To remove an app from a folder, press down the app to highlight it, then move it to a different location.

- To delete a folder, press hard on the folder and click **Delete Folder.** All the apps in the folder will return to the Apps screen.

Show All Apps on the Home Screen
Eliminate the app screen and have all your app icons on the home screen instead.

- Tap and hold any empty space on the home screen until you see the settings option.
- Click ⚙ **Settings** and select **Home Screen Layout.**
- Choose **Home Screen Only** and click **Apply.**
- Swipe left or right on the home screen to see all your app icons.

App Screen Grid
Configure the layout of app icons on the app screen

- Tap and hold any empty space on the home screen until you see the settings option.
- Click ⚙ **Settings** & select **App Screen Grid**
- Choose an option and press **Save**

Home Screen Grid
Configure the layout of app icons on the home screen

- Tap and hold any empty space on the home screen until you see the settings option.

- Click ⚙ **Settings** and select **Home Screen Grid**
- Choose an option and press **Save**

Folder Grid
Configure the layout of folders on the home/ app screen

- Tap and hold any empty space on the home screen until you see the settings option.
- Click ⚙ **Settings,** select **Folder Grid,** & choose an option.

Add Media Page to HOME screen
Add the Samsung Free feature to the home screen to enjoy content like live TV, games, news articles, and more.

- Tap and hold any empty space on the home screen until you see the settings option.
- Click ⚙ **Setting,** click **Add Media Page to Home Screen,** turn on the service and select an option.

- Once active, go home and swipe right to the end to use the Samsung Free service.

Lock Home Screen Layout

Use this setting to prevent someone from changing the arrangement of icons on the home screen

- Tap and hold any empty space on the home screen until you see the settings option.

- Click ⚙ **Setting** and turn on **Lock Home Screen Layout.**

Add New Apps to Home Screen

If disabled, new apps will only be added on the app screen.

- Tap and hold any empty space on the home screen until you see the settings option.

- Click ⚙ **Setting** and turn on **Add New Apps to Home Screen.**

Hide Apps

Hide apps from appearing in the app and home screen. Repeat these steps to unhide the app.

- Tap and hold any empty space on the home screen until you see the settings option.

- Click ⚙ **Setting,** click **Hide App** and select the apps you want to hide or deselect apps to unhide them.

Swipe Down for Notification Panel
To see the notification panel, you would need to swipe down from the topmost part of any screen, including the home screen. This option allows you to swipe down from any part of the home screen to open the notification panel

- Tap and hold any empty space on the home screen until you see the settings option.

- Click ⚙ **Setting** and turn on **Swipe Down for Notification Panel**

Rotate to Landscape Mode
Configure your phone to automatically switch from portrait to landscape when you rotate the home screen.

- Tap and hold any empty space on the home screen until you see the settings option.
- Click ⚙ **Setting** and turn on **Rotate to Landscape Mode**
- **Down for**

Chapter 7: Using Apps

Swipe upwards on your home screen to go to the App screen

Uninstall or Disable Apps

Note that not all preloaded apps can be uninstalled.

- Go to the app screen, press down on the app until it wiggles, then select **Uninstall** or **Disable.**

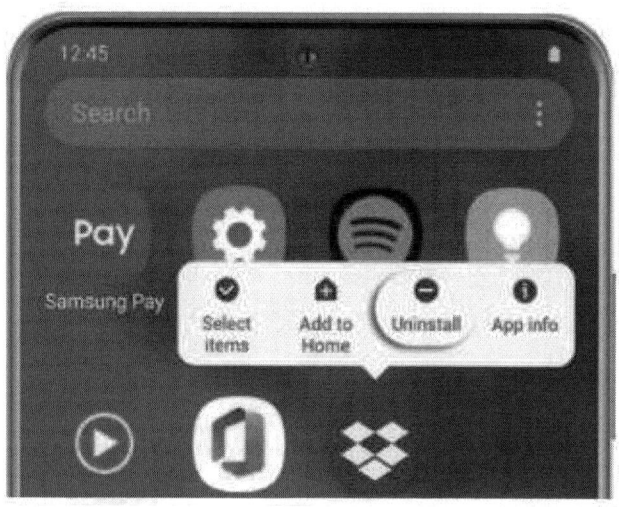

Find Apps

- Go to the Apps Screen & click **Search.**
- You will find a refined list as you type in the app names.
- Click the desired app to open it.

Sort Apps
Arrange the apps alphabetically or manually

- Click ⋮ at the top of the App Screen
- Click **Sort** and choose either **Custom Order** (manually arrange apps) or **Alphabetical Order** (arrange alphabetically).

If you selected Custom Order, you could use the steps below to clean up empty spaces

- Click ⋮ at the top of the App Screen and select **Clean Up Pages.**

Choose Default Apps
Select a default app for using certain features and functions on your device.

- Open **Settings** and click **Apps.**
- Click **Choose Default Apps,** select individual options like Browser, Phone, etc., and select the default app for those options.

Game Booster

Enjoy your gaming experience as the device optimizes the performance of the phone while playing games.

- Open one game and swipe upward from the bottom of your screen to display the navigation bar. You will see the options below on the far left & right sides of your screen:
    - Click **Touch Protection** to lock your screen and prevent accidental taps.
    - Click **Game Booster** to customize other options like blocking the navigation bar, performance monitoring, screenshots, and screen touches.

Samsung App Settings

See all the Samsung apps and customize the different settings.

- Open **Settings** and click **Apps**.
- Click **Samsung App Settings,** click an app and customize the setting to suit your need.

Chapter 8: Screen Record and Screen Capture

Screen record records activities on your screen while screen capture takes a screenshot of your screen and allows you to draw, write, crop, or share the screenshot.

Screen Record

- Swipe down from the topmost part of your screen two times to go to the Quick Settings panel.

- Press ⦿ to start screen recorder. Choose a sound setting and then click **Start Recording.**

- The recording will begin at the end of the countdown.

- Tap ✏ to write on the recording.

- Tap ▼ to display the S Pen pointer on your screen. This option is only for S22 Ultra. The S

Pen must be detached from the device to use this option.

- Tap 👤 to add yourself to the recording using the selfie camera.

- Tap ⏹ to stop recording. The video will be stored in your gallery.

Change Screen Recorder Settings
- Go to the Settings app and click **Advanced Features.**
- Click **Screenshots and Screen Recorder** and scroll to **Screen Recorder** to change the desired settings: Sounds, Video Quality, Selfie Video Size, Show Taps, and Touches.

Capture a Screenshot
You can capture screenshots in two ways:

1. Press the Volume Down key and the Side key simultaneously (Key capture).
2. Place the edge of your hand on one end of your screen and swipe the hand to the right or left

of the screen to capture the screen (Swipe capture). Note that you may need to turn on this option with the steps below:

> Go to the Settings app and click **Advanced Features.**

> Select **Motions and gestures,** then switch on the **Palm swipe to Capture** button.

After you take a screenshot, you will find a toolbar at the end of the image.

- Click to capture more content on a long page like a webpage.
- Tap to draw on the picture or crop a part of it.
- Click # to include tags in the image for easy find in the future.
- Tap to share the image.

Turn on the Screenshot Toolbar

Use the steps below to turn on the screenshot toolbar if you cannot find it at the bottom immediately after taking a screenshot.

- Go to the Settings app and click **Advanced Features.**
- Click **Screenshots and Screen Recorder** and turn on the **Screenshot Toolbar** button.

Screenshot Settings

- Go to the Settings app and click **Advanced Features.**
- Click **Screenshots and Screen Recorder**.
- Switch on **Hide Status and Navigation Bar** to exclude the navigation or status bars on your screenshot
- Switch on **Delete Shared Screenshots** to allow the device to automatically delete shared screenshots.

- Click **Screenshot Format** and choose a format for the saved screenshots: **PNG** or **JPG.**

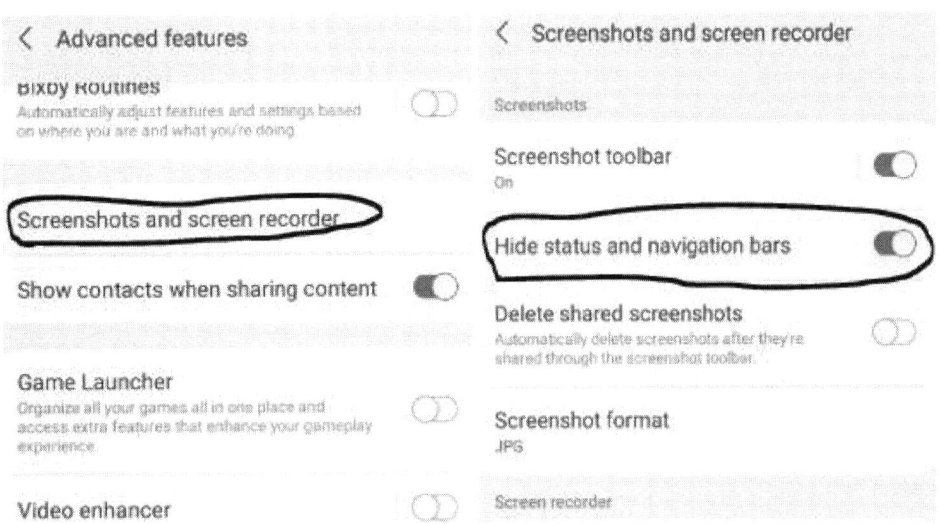

Chapter 9: Edge Panel

By default, the edge panel is located at the extreme right or left side of your screen. It houses different features and apps for quick access. Add your favorite apps to this panel to access them quickly in the future.

Turn on Edge Panel
- Go to the Settings app and click **Display.**
- Click **Edge Panel** and turn on the switch.
- Pull the edge panel button to the middle of your screen to open it.

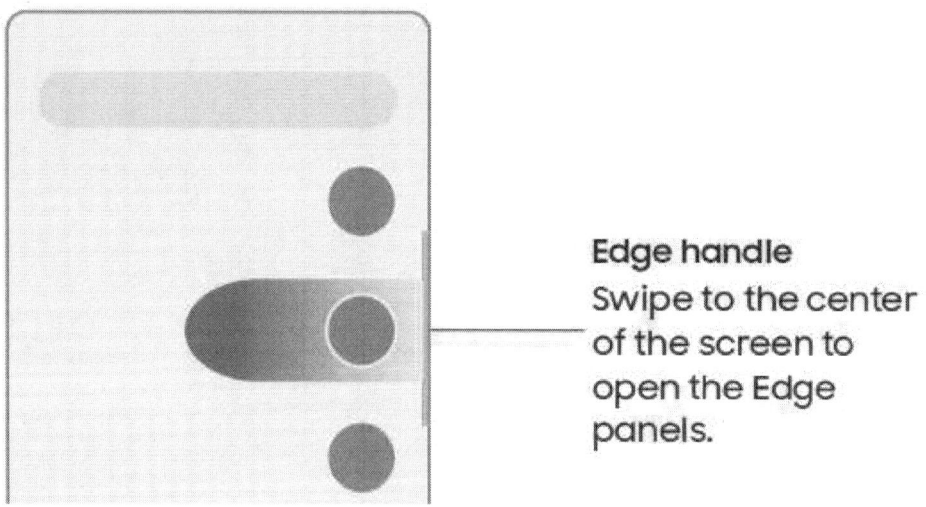

Edge handle
Swipe to the center of the screen to open the Edge panels.

Apps Panel
Add your favorite apps to the App panel.

- Pull out the edge handle, and swipe until you see the screen showing the apps (Apps panel).

- Click an app to open it. Or tap ☰, and press ⋮⋮⋮ to see a list of all the apps in the apps panel.

- You can also open more app windows in the pop-up view. Simply pull the app icon and drop it on the open screen.

Configure Apps Panel
Add/ remove apps from the apps panel.

- Pull out the edge handle, and swipe until you see the screen showing the apps (Apps panel).

- Tap ☰ and press ✎ to add or remove apps. Click apps on the left part of the screen to add them to the app panels or tap ⊖ on an app to remove it from the Apps panel.

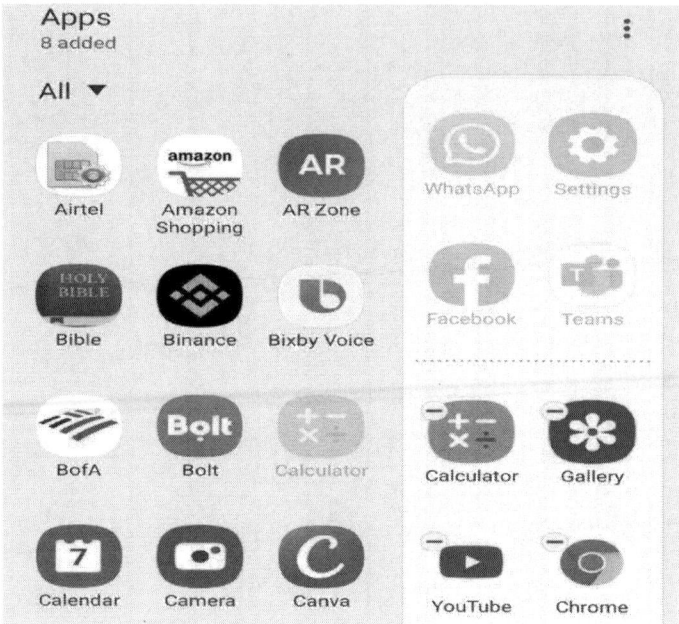

- To create a folder, pull one app from the ones on the left side and drop on top an app on the right side.
- Pull the app icons around to modify the order.
- Tap ⟨ to store your changes.

Configure Edge Panels
To customize the edge panel,

- Open **Settings** and click **Display**
- Click **Edge Panels** and select **Panels.**

- Select ✓ or deselect all the panels you want to add to or remove from the edge handle.
- Click **Edit** under compatible panels to add or remove features
- Tap 🔍 to search for available and installed panels.
- Click ⋮ and click **Reorder** to move the panels around. Or click **Uninstall** and tap ⊖ on a panel to delete it. Click **Hide on Lock Screen** to select panels that should be invisible on the lock screen.
- Tap ‹ to save changes.

Edge Panel Position and Style
Change the location of the Edge panel handle.

- Open **Settings** and click **Display**
- Click **Edge Panels** and select **Handles.**

- Move the ⬍ icon up or down to change its position.
- Click **Position** and choose to have the handle either on the right or left.
- Turn on the **Lock Handle Position** ⬤ switch to prevent movement of the handle outside this setting screen.
- Click a color under **Style** to use for the edge handle.
- Pull the **Transparency** slider to adjust the handle's transparency.
- Drag the **Size** slider to change the size of the handle.
- Drag the **Width** handle to change the handle's width.

Chapter 10: Galaxy S22 Ultra S Pen

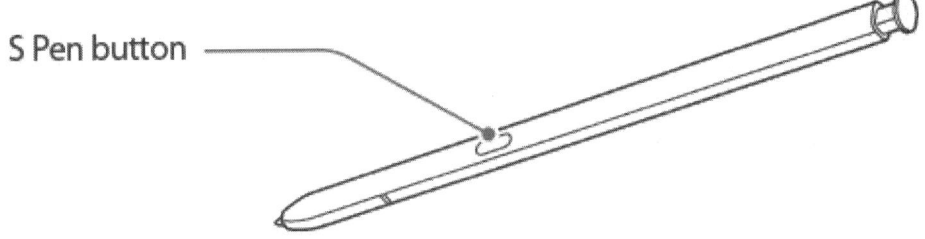

The S22 Ultra comes with an S Pen that can serve various functions. You can use the pen to control apps remotely, take pictures, and lots more.

Store and Detach the S Pen
Follow the steps below to remove the S Pen from its slot.

- Push the bottom of the S Pen to unlock it from the slot, then pull it out gently.
- To store the pen, push it into the pen slot until it clicks into position.

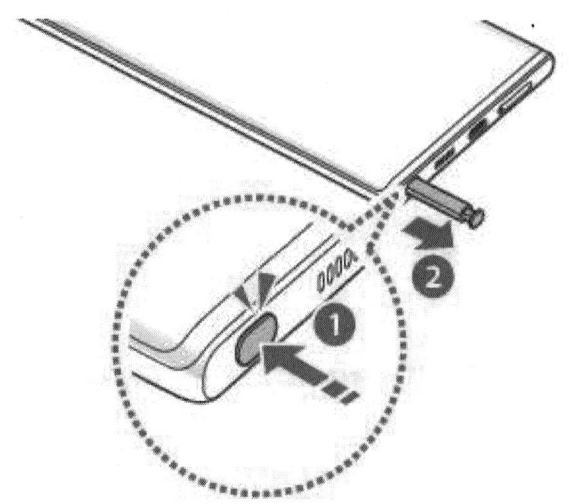

Charge the S Pen

You need to ensure the S Pen is charged before using it for any activity.

- Return the S Pen to its slot to start charging it. If you turned off the Air Action feature, the S Pen would only begin charging when charging the S22.

Reset Your S Pen

You will need to reset the S Pen if it loses connection to the S22. To do this,

- Return the pen to its slot

- Go to the Settings app and click **Advanced Features.**

- Click **S Pen** → **Air Action**, tap ⋮ and select **Reset S Pen.**

- Wait for the connection process to finish before you pull out the S Pen.

Air Actions

There are lots of remote controls attached to the S Pen. For instance,

- Press and hold the S Pen button and lift the S Pen up at the same time to increase audio volume or lift the S Pen down to reduce volume.

- Press and hold the S Pen button to turn on apps like the camera app.

- Open the camera app and press the S Pen button one time to take your picture.

To use this Air Action feature, note the following tips

- Charge the S Pen before using Air Action.
- Once you remove the pen from its slot, you will see the ✏ icon at the top of the screen. The icon will change to ✏ if the S Pen is disconnected from the phone either because the pen is far from your S Pen or there are some obstacles or interference between the S22 and the S Pen. Re-insert the S Pen into its slot to reconnect it with the S22 and activate the Air Action features.

Hold the S Pen Button Shortcut

Assign an action that should happen when you touch and hold the pen button.

- Open **Settings** and click **Advanced Feature.**
- Click **S Pen** and select **Air Actions.**
- Press **Hold Down Pen Button to** and turn on the ⬤ switch.
- Then assign a function to the shortcut.

Anywhere Actions

These are shortcuts you can customize to access certain features when holding the S Pen and making five gestures: swipe down, up, right, left, or shake. Follow the steps below to customize the shortcuts.

- Open **Settings** and click **Advanced Feature.**
- Click **S Pen** and select **Air Actions.**
- Scroll to **Anywhere Actions** and select a **Gesture** icon to customize its shortcut.

Action	Gesture
Back	Left to right
Recents	Right to left
Home	Up and down
Smart select	Down and up
Screen write	Zigzag

App Actions

Use different S Pen features for different apps. Use this setting to customize S Pen actions for each app

- Open **Settings** and click **Advanced Feature.**
- Click **S Pen** and select **Air Actions.**
- Select an app to see the shortcuts available, then turn on the switch to use those shortcuts for the identified app.

Take Pictures with the S Pen

With the S Pen, no need to set a timer to take a picture when your device is placed at a distance. To turn on this setting,

- Go to the Settings app and click **Advanced Features.**
- Click **S Pen** → **Air Action** and then turn on the Air Actions button.

once done, follow the steps below to take your picture:

- Open the camera app and position your device.
- Then press the pen button one time to take the picture.
- Press and continue to hold the pen button to take multiple pictures.
- Swing the S Pen to the right or left while holding the S Pen button to change the camera shooting mode.
- Push the S Pen two times to switch between the rear and back cameras.

General App Actions

Customize some general actions for apps that are not included in the app action list, like camera and media apps.

- Open **Settings** and click **Advanced Feature.**

- Click **S Pen** and select **Air Actions.**
- Click an action under **General App Action** to customize it.

Air Command

Air Command provides quick access to apps that you use frequently.

- Remove the S Pen from its slot, hold it close to your screen and push the pen button to launch the Air command panel. Or simply use your S Pen to tap the ⊘(Air Command) icon.
- Then choose the app or function you wish to access on the Air command panel. I have explained how to use these functions below.
- Note that pulling out the S Pen will not show the Air Command panel if your screen is locked and you have a screen lock method.

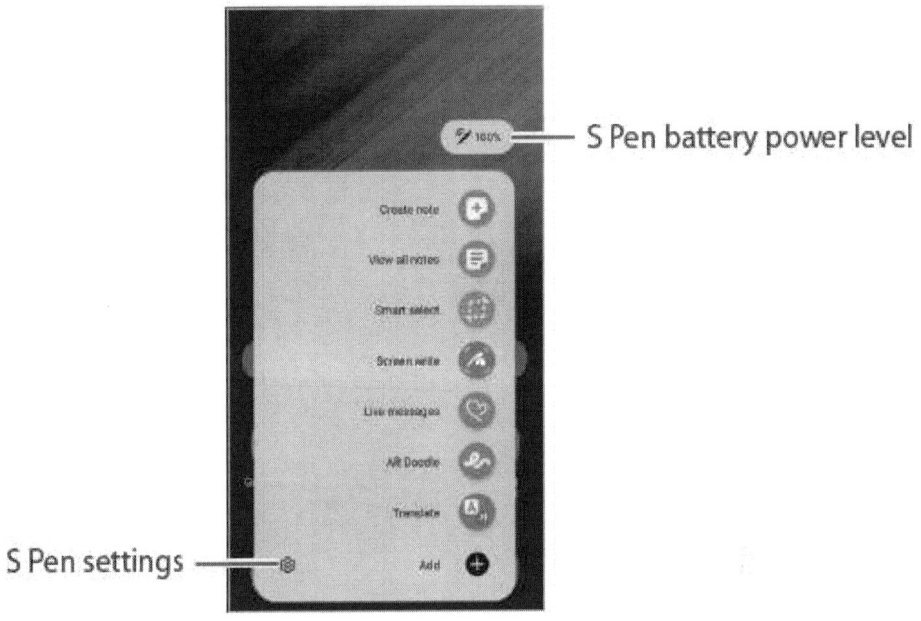

Air Command Icon

This ⬤ icon remains on your screen even after you close the Air Command panel.

- Use your S Pen to tap the Air Command icon to launch the Air Command panel.
- Drag the ⬤ icon to change its location.
- To delete the icon, drag the ⬤ icon and drop it on the **Remove** option at the top of your screen.

Turn on the Air Command Icon

Use the steps below to turn on the Air Command icon if it isn't yet showing on your screen.

- Go to the Settings app and click **Advanced Features.**

- Click **S Pen** and then turn on the **Show Air Command Icon** button.

- Hover your pen over the ⊘ to view Air Actions features on compatible apps,

Smart Select

Select an area on your screen to share, save, and more. You can also create a GIF from a video recording using the Smart Select option.

- Open the content you wish to capture, then launch the Air Command panel and choose the **"Smart Select"** option.

- Choose any shape icon showing on the toolbar, then pull the pen across the item you want to select.

- Once done selecting, you will find new buttons to customize your selection:
  - Click ⌖ to automatically modify the looks of the selected area
  - Click T to copy out the text in the selected area
  - Click ✎ to draw or write on the area.
  - Select **Pin/Insert** to pin the area to your phone screen.
  - Click ⩿ to share with others
  - Click ⤓ to store the selected area on your phone.

Capture Parts of a Video
Select a part of a video and turn it into a GIF.

- Open the content you wish to capture, then launch the Air Command panel and choose the "**Smart Select**" option.
- Press [GIF] on the toolbar.

- Set the size and placement of the capturing area.
- Choose any shape icon showing on the toolbar, then pull the pen across the item you want to select.

Adjust the position.

Drag a corner of the frame to resize.

- Play the video and click **Ready** once you are ready to capture. Note that the sound will not be included in the capture.
- Click **Stop** to finish.
- Once done selecting, you will find new buttons to customize the selection:
    - Click ✐ to draw or write on the area.
    - Click ⤳ to share with others

➢ Click ⌄ to store the selected area on your phone. Tap ▶ to play the recording before saving it.

Screen Write
This is another way to take a screenshot using the Air Command feature.

88

- Open the content you wish to capture, then launch the Air Command panel and choose the "**Screen Write**" option.
- The device will automatically take the screenshot, and you will see the editing bars at the bottom.
  - Click ✏ to write on the area.
  - Click ⋖ to share with others
  - Click ⬇ to store the screenshot on your phone.

Live Messages

Record your screen as you draw or handwrite a live message, then turn the message into an animated file.

- Launch the Air Command panel and choose the "**Live**
- **Messages**" option.
- Set your background image and click **Start Drawing** or **Done.**

- Then use the S Pen to draw or write your message on the screen.
- Click **Done** to finish, and the message will be saved as a video or animated GIF file in your phone gallery.
- To share, select **Share,** and choose a method.

Translate
Translate words from one language to another.

- Open the text you want to translate, launch the Air Command panel, and choose the "**Translate**" option.

- Choose the from and to languages on the translator button on top of your screen. Tap ⓣ or 🗐 to change the text between sentences and words.

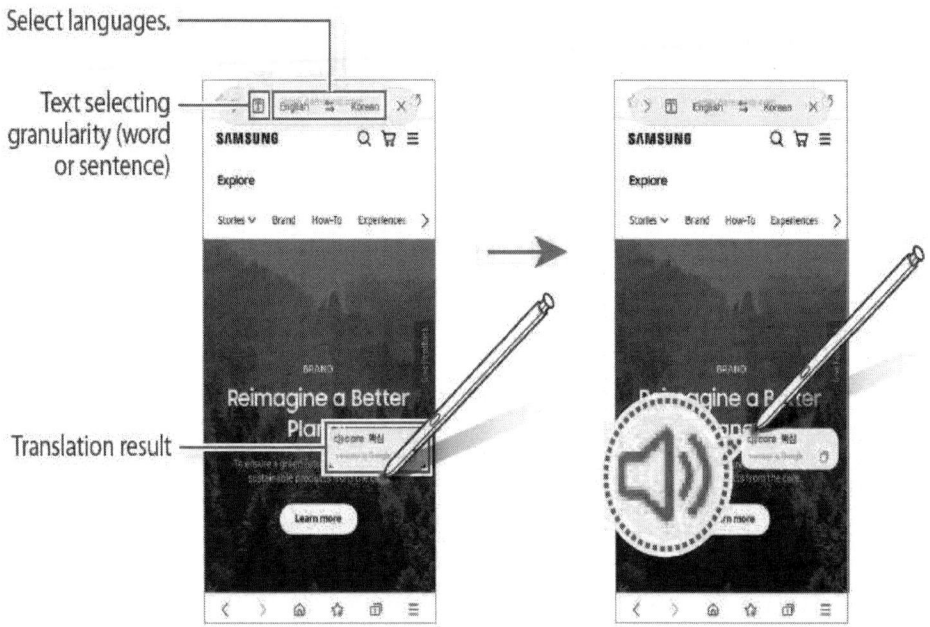

- Hold your S Pen above the text you wish to translate, and the translated version will automatically show.
- Click 🔊 to play the pronunciation of the initial text.

Note that this feature isn't available for all languages.

Glance

This feature allows you to minimize an app to a thumbnail while viewing another page and then switch between both apps. For instance, while the map app is open, click **Glance** in the Air Command panel to minimize it to the bottom of your screen as you view a webpage, then hold the S Pen over the minimized app to quickly search for places while the webpage is open.

- Open an app, launch the Air Command panel, and choose the **"Glance"** option to minimize the screen for that app.
- To use the first app while viewing a second one, hold your S Pen above the minimized app to open the app in full screen. Move your S pen away from your screen to minimize the app again

- To close the app, press firmly on the app thumbnail and pull it on top of the **Remove** button at the top of your screen.

Write on Calendar
Write or draw on your calendar.

- Launch the Air Command panel and choose the "**Write on Calendar**" option.
- Use the S Pen to fill in details on your calendar, then tap **Save.** Tap ✎ to edit the calendar entry.

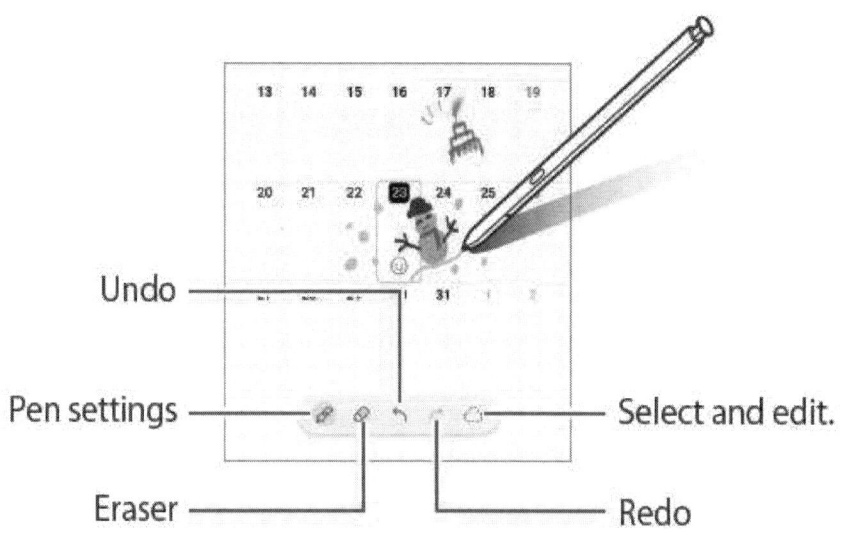

S Pen to Text

Convert handwritten words into text using the S Pen. To turn on this setting,

- Go to the Settings app and click **Advanced Features.**
- Click **S Pen → S Pen to Text** and then turn on the ⬤ switch.
- Once done, use the S Pen to enter your words in a text input field, and the handwritten words will be converted to text.

Air View

Use this option to preview content on your screen or access information in a different window. Hold the S Pen above the item you want to preview. Follow the steps below to turn on this setting:

- Go to the Settings app and click **Advanced Features.**
- Click **S Pen** and turn on the **Air View** ⬤ switch.

Pen Select

To select text and other content using the S Pen,

- Open the content you want to select. Press & hold the Pen button while you drag the S Pen over the items you want to select.

- Then share your selection or copy and paste it into a different app.

Screen Off Memo

Write memos while your screen is asleep.

- With your screen on sleep mode, remove the S pen or hold it above the screen and push the pen button.

- Write your memo and use buttons on your screen to customize

    ➢ Tap ○ to change color. Tap ◇ to use an eraser, then tap the icon twice to clean all you wrote.

    ➢ Tap ✎ to use the pen feature. Tap it two times to modify line thickness.

- Click **Save** or return the pen to its slot to save the memo to Samsung Notes.

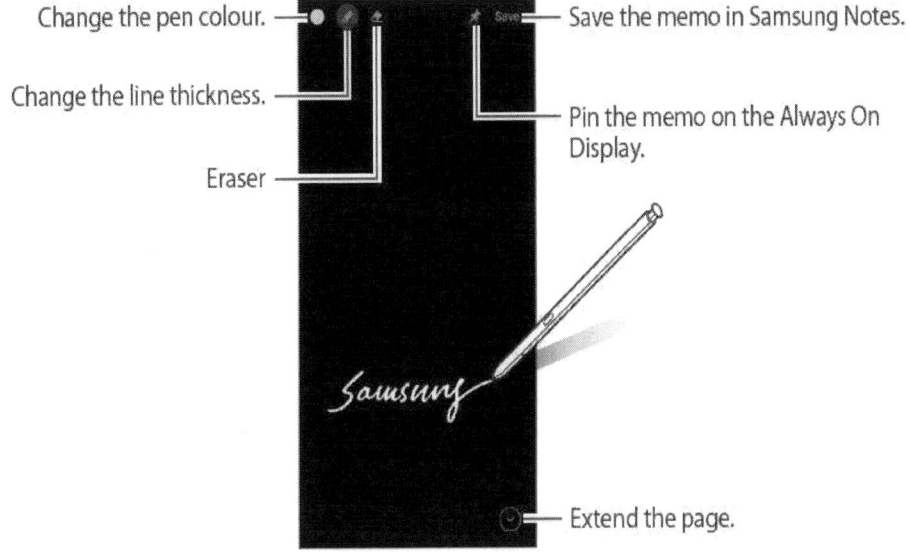

Follow the steps below to turn on this feature:

- Go to the Settings app and click **Advanced Features.**

- Click **S Pen,** select **Screen Off Memo,** and switch on the button.

Pin a Screen Off Memo on the Always on Display

You can pin your memo on the locked screen's Always on Display.

- Write your screen-off memo, then tap 📌 and select **Pin to Always on Display.** The pinned memo will remain unsaved.

- Double click the pinned memo to edit it.

- Double click ⊛ to reduce the pinned memo to an icon. The reduced memo will show as 📌 icon. Click the 📌 icon to expand the memo.

Unlock Your Screen with the S Pen

To use this option, the S Pen must have been connected at the time the screen was locked. Press the S Pen button to unlock the screen. Follow the steps below to turn on this setting:

- Go to the Settings app and click **Advanced Features.**

- Click **S Pen,** select **S Pen Unlock.**

- Click **Use S Pen Unlock,** then press **OK.**

The screen lock method must be set before you can use this option.

Show Pointer When Hovering

- Open the **Settings** app and click **Advanced Features.**

- Select **S Pen** and turn on **Show Pointer When Hovering** to see the pen pointer on your screen when the s pen is close to the screen.

Allow Multiple S Pen
Use more than one pen at the same time.

- Open the **Settings** app and click **Advanced Features.**

- Select **S Pen** and turn on **Allow Multiple S Pen**

Keep S Pen Connected
This setting will ensure the S Pen is always ready for use whenever you pull it out of its slot.

- Open the **Settings** app and click **Advanced Features.**

- Select **S Pen** and turn on **Keep S Pen Connected.**

The Appearance of the Air Command
Customize the look of the Air Command menu

- Open the **Settings** app and click **Advanced Features.**
- Select **S Pen** and click **Menu Style.**

Shortcut Settings
Set up S Pen functions, apps, and features for the Air command menu.

- Open the **Settings** app and click **Advanced Features.**
- Select **S Pen** and click **Shortcut.**

Open Air command with Pen Button
See the Air command icon when you hold the pen above your screen and push the pen button.

- Open the **Settings** app and click **Advanced Features.**

- Select **S Pen** and turn on **Open Air command with Pen Button.**

Warn if S Pen is Left Behind

Configure your phone to beep you once you start to move away from the S Pen

- Open the **Settings** app and click **Advanced Features.**
- Select **S Pen** and turn on **Warn if S Pen is Left Behind.**

When S Pen is Removed

What should happen when you pull out the S Pen? Set it up here:

- Open the **Settings** app and click **Advanced Features.**
- Select **S Pen** and click **When S Pen is removed.**

S Pen Sound Customization

Make your phone release sounds when you remove and insert the pen or write using the pan.

- Open the **Settings** app and click **Advanced Features.**
- Select **S Pen** and turn on **Sound.**
- Turn on **Vibrations** to also feel vibrations for these actions.

Chapter 11: Biometric Security

Face Recognition
Face recognition uses your facial image to unlock your phone and verify your identity.

- Open **Settings** and click **Biometrics and Security.**
- Click **Face Recognition** and use the prompt on your screen to finish setting up.

Delete Face Data
Remove any saved face data

- Open **Settings** and click **Biometrics and Security.**
- Click **Face Recognition** and tap **Remove Face Data.**

Add Alternative Appearance
Record your face with accessories you wear often.

- Open **Settings** and click **Biometrics and Security.**

- Click **Face Recognition,** tap **Add Alternative Appearance to Enhance Recognition,** and use the prompt on your screen to finish setting up.

Face Unlock
Enable or disable to use or not use saved face data to unlock your screen.

- Open **Settings** and click **Biometrics and Security.**
- Click **Face Recognition** and turn on **Face Unlock** switch.

Stay on Lock Screen Until Swipe
Configure the phone to remain on the lock screen even after you have used the appropriate security method to unlock the phone.

- Open **Settings** and click **Biometrics and Security.**
- Click **Face Recognition** and turn on **Stay on Lock Screen Until Swipe** switch.

Other Face Recognition Management
- Open **Settings,** click **Biometrics and Security,** and tap **Face Recognition**
- Turn on **Faster Recognition** to configure your device to fasten the identification process.
- Turn on **Require Open Eyes** to configure your device to recognize the face only when your eyes are clearly open.
- Turn on **Brighten Screen** to improve the screen lighting whenever you need to unlock with your face.

Fingerprint Scanner
Here is another way to verify your identity

- Open **Settings** and click **Biometrics and Security.**
- Click **Fingerprints** and use the prompt on your screen to add fingerprints.

Add, Delete and Rename Fingerprints

Add new fingerprints up to five or delete one of the added fingerprints

- Open **Settings** and click **Biometrics and Security.**
- Click **Fingerprints** and click **Add Fingerprints** to add a new one.
- To remove, tap the one you want to delete and press **Remove.**
- To check the finger you used for each number, click **Check Added Fingerprints,** and scan your fingerprints to identify the prints that belong to a number/ name.
- To name, tap the one you want to rename, enter the new name, and press **Save.**

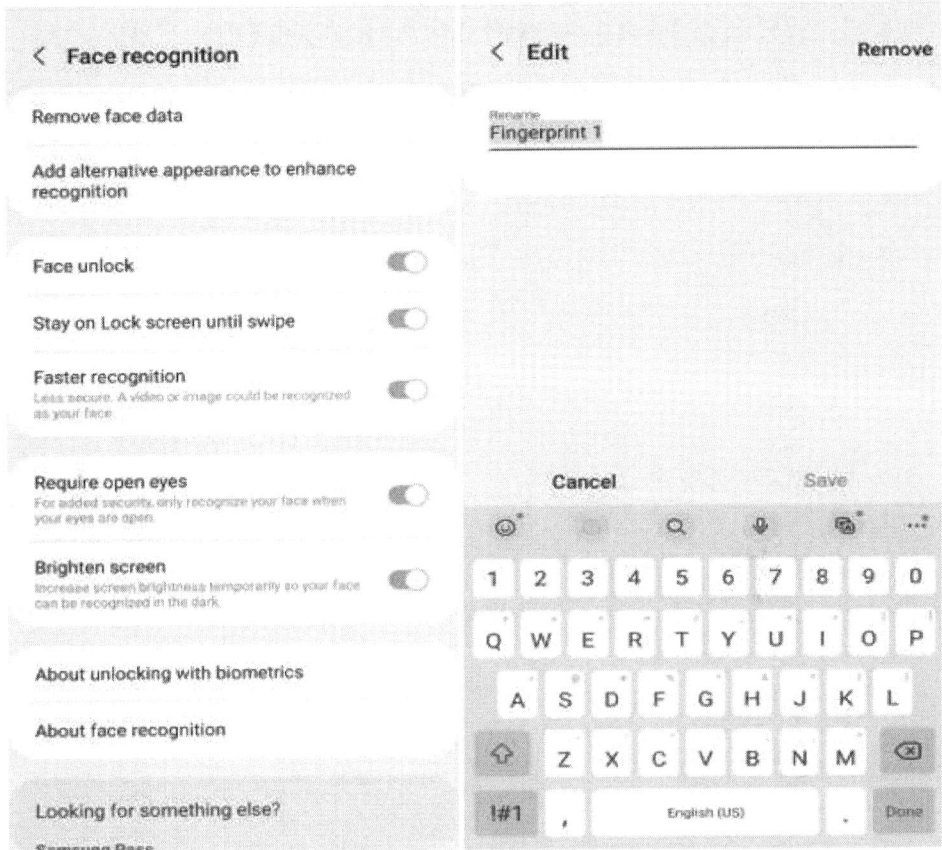

Fingerprint Verification Settings

Use registered fingerprints for identity verification in supported apps and features.

- Open **Settings,** click **Biometrics and Security,** and tap **Fingerprints.**
- Turn on **Fingerprint Unlock** switch to use it on the locked screen.

- Turn on **Fingerprint Always On** switch to scan your fingerprint even with a locked screen.

- Click **Show Icon When Screen is On** and select when you want to see the fingerprint icon.

- Turn on **Show Animation When Unlocking** switch to see an animation when using this verification method.

Biometric Settings
Customize your biometric preferences.

- Open **Settings,** click **Biometrics and Security,** and tap **More Biometrics Settings.**

- Turn on **Show Unlock Transition Effect** switch to see a transaction effect when unlocking the S22 with any biometric option.

- Click **Biometrics Security Patch** to see the biometric feature software version

Security Update

See the last time the security software was updated and check for new updates.

- Open **Settings,** click **Biometrics and Security,** then click **Security Update.** You will find a **Download** button if there is a new update.

Private Share

Prevent recipients from resharing files you shared with them privately and set expiration dates for the file sharing.

- Open **Settings,** click **Biometrics and Security,** then click **Private Share.**
- **Agree** to the terms, and give access to the app
- To share a file privately, click **Share Files,** select the item folder, tick all the items you want to share, and tap **Done.**
- In the **Select Recipients** screen, click ⚙, click **Expiration Date** to choose an expiry

date, then click **Done.** You may also turn on **Add Private Share to App Screen** to have an app icon for this feature.

- Press ⟨ to return to the recipient screen, select your recipient, and click **Send.**
- The recipient would be unable to access the file after the expiry date.

Turn on Find My Mobile
This setting allows you to track your device online, lock the device or remotely erase its content. This is for times when the device is lost or stolen. You need to turn on the Google Location service to use this feature. Follow the steps below to turn on Find My Mobile:

- Open **Settings,** click **Biometrics and Security,** then click **Find My Mobile.**
- Tap the ⬤ switch to turn on the future and sign in to your Samsung account. Then you will find the options below:

> Turn on the **Remote Unlock** switch to permit Samsung to store your secure code settings and allow you to control your smartphone remotely. This is helpful for times when you forget your unlock method.

> Turn on **Send Last Location** to configure your phone to send the phone's last location to the Samsung server once your phone battery goes under a defined level.

Secure Folder
Create a secure folder where you store items that you want to keep private.

- Open **Settings,** click **Biometrics and Security,** then click **Secure Folder.**
- Click **Continue,** tap **Continue** again and wait for the folder to be created
- Select a lock type for the secure folder and enter the corresponding details.

- To add apps to the folder, click ✚, select the apps, and tap **Add.**

- To add files, click ⋮, select **Add Files,** click the file folder, select the files, and press **Done.**

Secure Folder Settings
After you have turned on the secure folder, follow the guide below to configure its settings

- Open **Settings,** click **Biometrics and Security,** then click **Secure Folder.**

- Click **Lock Type** to change your security method

- To auto-lock the folder, click **Auto Lock Secure Folder** and choose an option

- Click **Notifications and Data** to customize notifications for apps inside the secure folder

Access Secure Folder
- Open **Settings,** click **Biometrics and Security,** then click **Secure Folder.**

- Turn on **Add Secure Folder to Apps Screen** to have an app icon for the secure folder.
- Then go to the app screen and find the Secure Folder app icon.

Set Up SIM Card Lock

Lock your SIM card with a PIN so that someone else would not have access to the card on another device.

- Open **Settings,** click **Biometrics and Security,** then click **Other Security Settings.**
- Click **Set Up SIM Card Lock** and turn on the **Lock SIM Card** button. You will be required to put your current card PIN to continue.
- Click **Change SIM Card PIN** to use a different PIN for the SIM card.

Install Unknown Apps

The device, by default, will block the installation of apps from unknown third-party sources. To install these kinds of apps,

- Open **Settings,** click **Biometrics and Security,** then click **Install unknown apps.**
- Tap ⬤ beside listed apps to allow installations from them.

View Passwords

Hide passwords as you type or show them briefly. To set up,

- Open **Settings,** click **Biometrics and Security,** then click **Other Security Settings.**
- Then turn on **Make Passwords Visible**

Pin Windows

Pin an open app to your screen to stop people from viewing features outside of the app you pinned.

Note that pinning an app would block features like messaging and calling. To pin,

- Open **Settings,** click **Biometrics and Security,** then click **Other Security Settings.**
- Click **Pin Window,** turn on the switch, and then turn **Ask for PIN before Unpinning** off or on.

To use,

- Open an app and click the **Recents** app button.
- Click the icon for the app you want to pin and select **Pin This App.**
- To close the feature, press and hold down your screen until you see the back button. If you turned on the Ask for Pin option, you would need to put the PIN to continue.

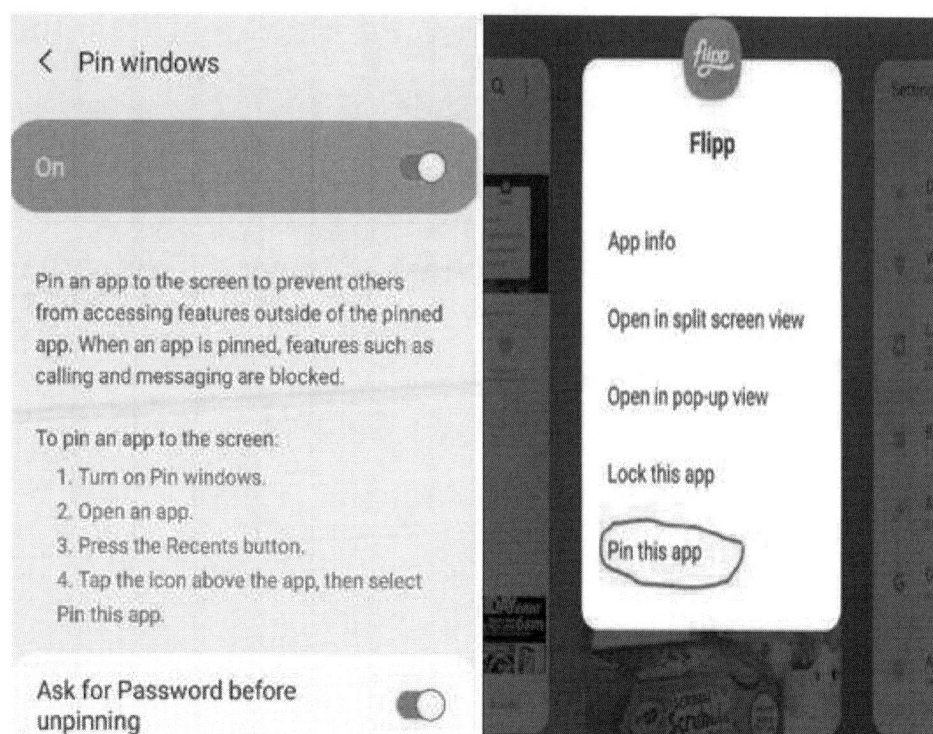

115

Chapter 12: Contacts App

Create and manage contacts on your S22.

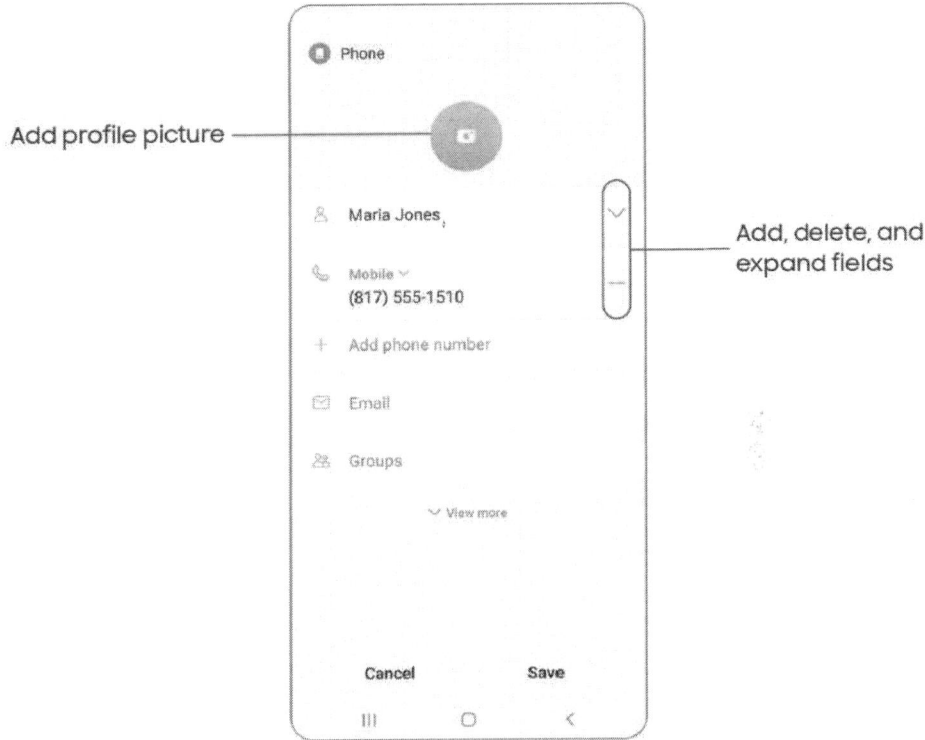

Create New Contact

To save a new phone number,

- Open the Contacts app and press +.
- Choose an option for storing the contact, enter the contact details, and press **Save**.

Import Contact

Import contacts to your S22 from other storage.

- Open the Contacts app and press ≡.
- Select **Manage Contacts → Import or Export Contacts,** then click **Import**
- Use the steps on your screen to import desired contacts.

Sync Contacts with Your Web Accounts

Sync the contacts on your S22 with the contacts stored in your web accounts like the Samsung account so that you would have an up-to-date contact list.

- Go to the Settings app and click **Accounts and Backup.**
- Select **Manage Accounts** and choose an account.
- Click **Sync Account** and then turn on the **Contacts** switch.

Edit a Contact

Add a new number, change the name or other details for a contact.

- Open the **Contacts** app, touch the contact, and press ✎.
- Make your changes and tap **Save.**

Favorites

Contacts marked as favorites are located on the first part of the contact list for easy access

- Open the **Contacts** app, touch the contact and press ☆.
- Press ★ to remove the contact from Favorites.

Search for Contacts

To find a contact,

- Open the Contacts app and press 🔍 at the top of the page.
- Select the desired contact and then press any of the buttons below
    - ➢ 📞 to initiate a voice call
    - ➢ 📹 or 📹 to initiate video call

- ➢ 🅞 to compose a text message
- ➢ 🅞 to compose a new email

Share Contacts
- Open the Contacts app, press ⋮ & select **Share Contacts**
- Select the contacts and press **Share.**
- Click one option on your screen: **Share as Text** or **Share as File.**
- Then choose a sharing channel.

Delete Contacts
- Open the Contacts app, press ⋮ & select **Delete Contacts**
- Click all the contacts you want to delete and press **Delete.**
- To delete single contact, find the contact in the contact app, click **More,** and press **Delete.**

Show Contacts when Sharing Content
Turn on this feature so that your contacts will appear when sharing items from within an app.

- Open **Settings** and click **Advanced Features.**
- Click **Show Contacts when Sharing** and turn on the switch.

Create Groups
Add your friends, family, and acquaintances to different contact groups.

- Open the Contacts app, press ≡ & select **Groups.**
- Click **Create Group** and continue with the on-screen instructions
- Tap **Save** to finish.

Add or Remove Group Contacts
To remove a contact from a group,

- Open the Contacts app, press ≡ & select **Groups.**
- Click the group, touch and hold the contact you want to remove, then tap 🗑

- To add a contact to the group, press ✏, press **Add Member,** and click a contact to add to the group

- Tap **Done** and select **Save** to finish.

Send a Message to a Group

- Open the Contacts app, press ≡ & select **Groups.**

- Click the group, tap ⋮ and select **Send Message.**

Merge Duplicate Contacts

Often, we erroneously save the same contact multiple times. See steps to merge duplicate contacts

- Open the Contacts app, press ≡ & select **Manage Contacts.**

- Click **Merge Contacts,** select contacts and press **Merge.**

Delete a Group

- Open the Contacts app, press ≡ & select **Groups.**

- Click the group, tap ⋮ and select **Delete Group Only.** This action will delete the group and return the contacts to the app.

- To delete the group and its contact, select **Delete Group and Move Members to the Trash.**

Emergency Contacts

Anyone can call your emergency contacts even with your phone screen locked.

- Open **Settings** and click **Safety and Emergency.**

- Select **Emergency Contacts** and press ✎.

- Make the necessary additions and press **Save.**

Chapter 13: Phone App

Answer or make video & phone calls

Make Calls on S22

- Open the Phone app and press **Keypad.**
- Type the recipient's phone number, then tap for voice call, or tap or or for video call.

Call from Your Contact List or Call Logs
- Open the Phone app and press **Contacts** or **Recents.**
- Find the number or contact you wish to call and swipe right on the item to start your call.

Use the steps below to turn on this feature if deactivated.

- Click ⋮ and select **Settings.**
- Choose **Other Call Settings,** tap **Swipe to Call or Text** and turn on the ⬤ switch.

Set Speed Dial
Use the steps below to add a number to your speed dial

- Open the Phone app and press **Keypad.**
- Tap ⋮ → **Speed Dial Numbers.** The screen will show you reserved speed dial numbers.
- Tap ▼ by the left to choose a free number for the speed dial.

- Enter the phone number or contact name or press 👤 to search through your contact.
- To call a contact on speed dial, press and hold the speed dial number on your keypad until the call begins.

Remove a Number from Speed Dial
Follow the steps below to unassign a number from speed dial

- Open the Phone app, tap ⋮ and select **Speed Dial Numbers.**
- Tap ➖ beside the number you want to remove from speed dial.

Make International Calls
- Open the Phone app and press **Keypad.**
- Press and hold the 0 number to add the + sign, then insert the country code and number for the contact before you press 📞

Answer a Call

- Pull the 📞 icon on an incoming call outside the large circle to answer the call.

Reject a Call

- Pull the 🔽 icon on an incoming call outside the large circle to reject the call.
- To send a message while declining the call, pull the send message bar on the call screen upwards, then choose a message for the caller.

See the steps below to customize your rejection messages:

- Open the Phone app, tap ⋮ and select **Settings.**
- Click **Quick Decline Messages,** enter the new message, and tap ➕.

Make a Multi-Party Call
Add other people to an existing call

- Tap ➕ in the active call screen, enter the new number, and tap 📞.

- Once the call is answered, press ⤴ to swap between the two calls or tap ↠ to add the new call to the existing one.

Video Call Effects

Blur your background during a video call in compatible apps. To set this,

- Open the Settings app and click **Advanced Features.**

- Click **Video Call Effects** and tap ⊙ to turn on the feature.

- Select a background color under **Background Color** or click ➕ under **Background Image** to choose a picture to use as your background during a video call.

Block Phone Numbers

- Open the Phone app, tap ⋮ & select **Settings**.

- Click **Block Numbers,** choose **Contacts** or **Recents,** click the phone number or contact, and press **Done.**
- You may also click **Add Phone Number** to manually input a phone number. Tap ✚ once done.
- Toggle on the **Block Unknown/ Private Numbers** switch to block calls from persons that hide their caller ID.

You will not receive notifications on calls from blocked numbers but will find the call in the call log.

Wi-Fi Calling
This setting allows you to use your Wi-Fi to call.

- Open the Phone app, tap ⋮ and select **Settings.**
- Click **Wi-Fi Calling** and tap ⬤ to turn on the feature. Follow the on-screen prompts to finish.

Chapter 14: Messages App

Send and manage your message conversations.

Send New Message

- Open the ⬤Messages app and press ⬤ near the bottom of your screen.
- Enter Recipient(s) and type in your message.
- Press and hold the ⬤icon to record a voice message. Release the button to stop recording.
- Press ⬤ to deliver your message.

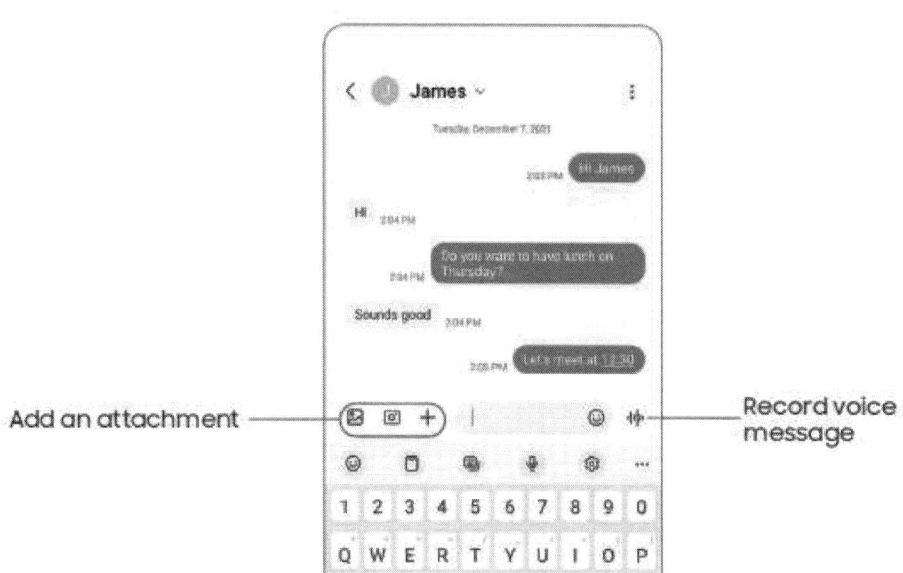

View Messages

- Click the **Conversation** tab in the Messages app home screen.
- Click on a message to open it. To respond, enter your reply in the message space and press ◉.
- Pinch or spread two fingers apart on the phone screen to increase or decrease the font size.

Sort Messages

Categories in the messaging app help you manage your message easily.

- Click the **Conversation** tab in the Messages app home screen.
- Press ✛, choose categories, and press **Done.**

To turn on the category switch if deactivated,

- Tap ⋮ in the Messages app, select **Settings** and then turn on the **Conversation Categories** button.

Delete Conversations

- Press and hold the message threads you wish to delete, then press 🗑 **Delete.**

- To delete a message in a thread, open the conversation thread and press down on the message you want to delete and select **Delete** in the pop-up. Tick other messages in that thread and then press **Delete** again.

Send SOS Messages

Share your location with designated contacts in an emergency. To turn on the feature,

- Go to the Settings app and click **Safety and Emergency.**

- Click **SOS Messages** and switch on the ⬤ button.

- You will be prompted to choose a contact or enter a phone number to receive your messages.

- Once done, return to the setting page and select the number of times you must push the side key for your S22 to send an SOS message: either **3 times** or **4 times**.

- Click on **Auto Call Someone** to designate someone you want to automatically call after sending an SOS message.

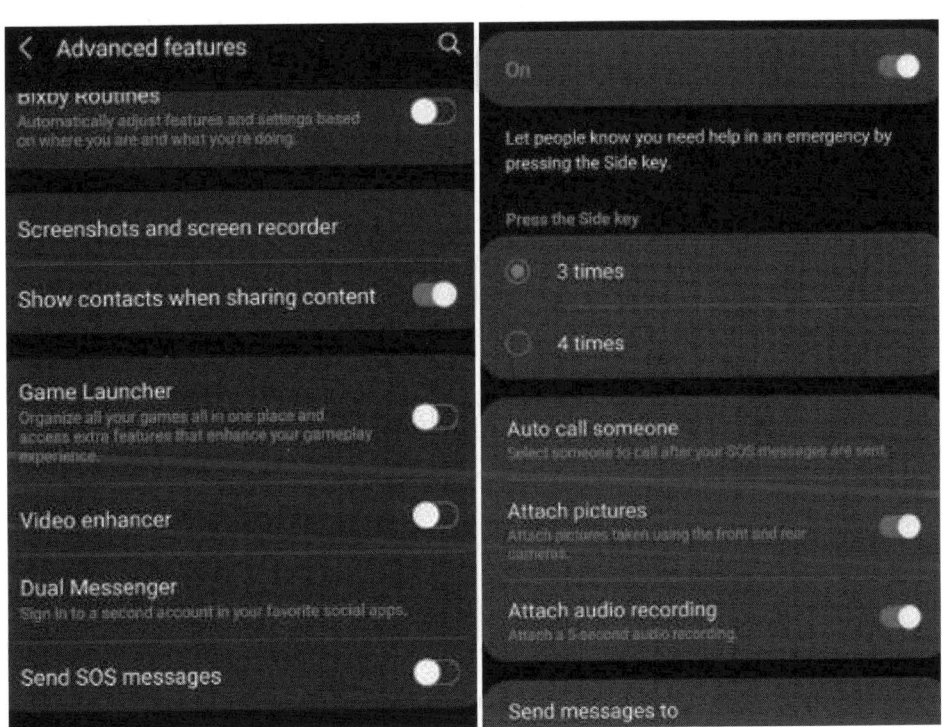

- Turn on **"Attach Pictures"** and **"Attach Audio Recording"** to include them in the SOS message.
- Once set, push the Side key four or three times, as preset, to send an SOS message.

Change Message Settings
- Tap ⋮ in the Messages app and select **Settings** to customize features like change notification settings, block unwanted messages and more.

Chapter 15: Calendar App

Connect all your calendars in the calendar app and have a holistic view of your dates and events.

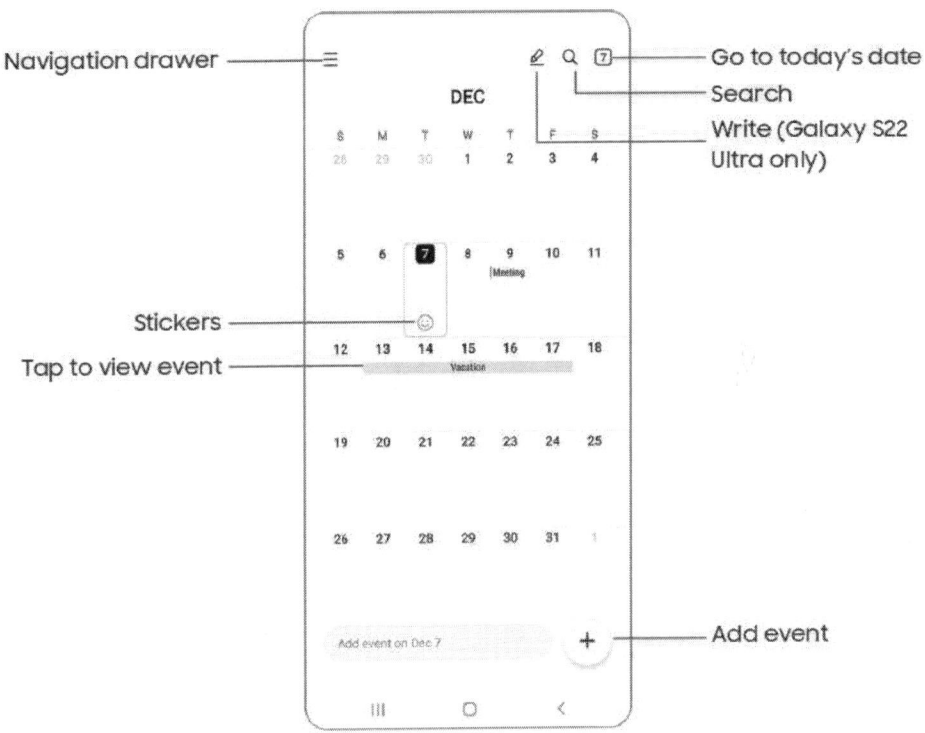

Add Accounts to Calendar App

- Open Calendar app and press ≡.

- Press **Manage Calendars,** tap + and choose a calendar account type.

- Input the account details and continue with the prompts.

Calendar Alert Style

Choose a different alert style for the calendar app.

- Open Calendar app and press .

- Press , select **Alert Style,** and choose a style:

  - ➢ **Strong:** you will see a full-screen alert and continue to hear the ring sound until you dismiss it.
  - ➢ **Light:** you will see a notification and hear a beep.
  - ➢ **Medium:** this is to see a full-screen alert and a beep.

- The style you select will determine the next option:

  - ➢ **Long Sound:** this is for you to select the alert sound to use for the Strong Alert style.

> **Short sound:** to select a desired alert sound for either the Medium or the Light alert styles.

Create an Event
Create new events in your calendar

- Tap ⊕ in the app, enter the event details and press **Save**.

Delete an Event
- Click the event, then click it again.

- Press 🗑 **Delete** and confirm your action.

Chapter 16: Internet

Bookmark your favorite web pages, share links, and lots more on the internet. This setting is for the Samsung browser

Access the Browser

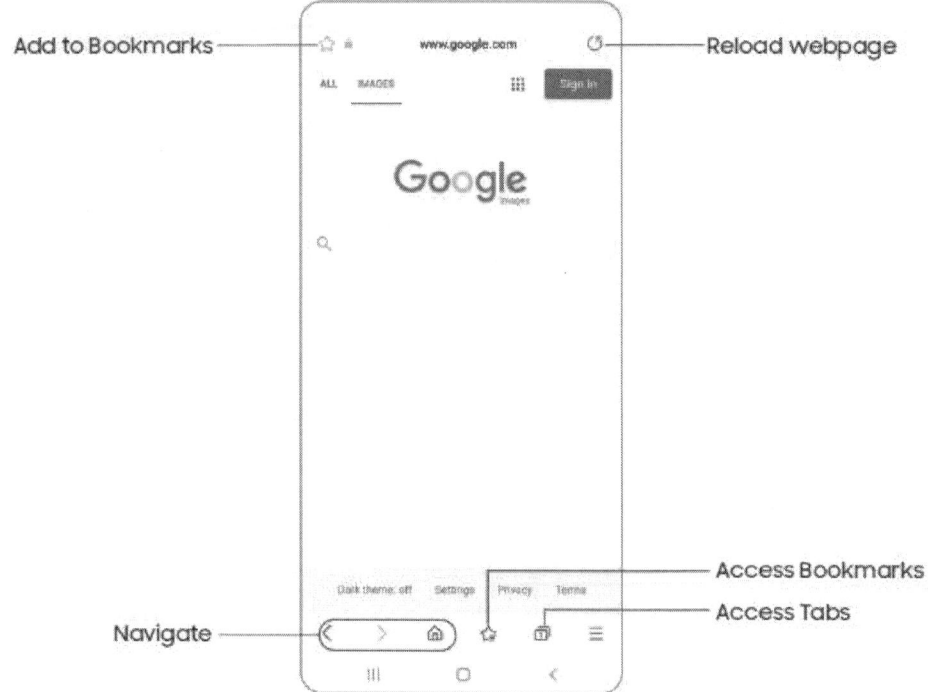

- Open the 🌀 internet app and input your keyword or site address on the search field, then press **Go** or **Enter** on your keypad.
- Drag your fingers downwards on the phone screen to reveal the toolbars.

- Swipe right and right on the address field to quickly navigate between open tabs.

Browser Tabs

Open multiple tabs to view different web pages simultaneously.

- Open the ⊙ internet app, press ▭ and select **New Tab**

- To close the tab, press ▭ and press ⊗ on that tab.

Create Bookmark

Bookmarking a page would help you find and access them quickly in the future.

- Tap ☆ on the opened page to add it to your bookmark.

Open a Bookmark

- Press ☆ in the browser and click a webpage to open it.

Save a Webpage

- Click ≡ on the opened webpage, select **Add Page To,** and choose an option on your screen:
    - ➢ **Bookmarks** – to add the page to bookmark
    - ➢ **Quick Access** – to see all your saved or commonly accessed webpages
    - ➢ **Home Screen** – add a shortcut of the webpage on your S22 home screen
    - ➢ **Saved Page** – save the web content on your device for easy access offline

Share Webpages

- click ≡ in the browser, select **Share** and continue with the prompts.

View/ Clear Browsing History
See all the pages you visited recently.

- To view history, click ≡ in the browser and select **History.**

- To clear the history, press ⋮, and select **Clear History.**

Browse on Secret Mode

The secret mode does not store your browsing or search history.

- In the browser, press ▢ and select **Turn on Secret Mode**
- Press **Start** to begin browsing.

To deactivate secret mode,

- In the browser, press ▢ and select **Turn off Secret Mode**

Note that you would be unable to use features like screen capture in secret mode.

Secret Mode Settings

You can create a password to lock the secret mode.

- In the browser, press ▢, and select ⋮.

- Then click **Secret Mode Settings** for the options below:
  - ➢ **Face** to unlock the secret page using face recognition
  - ➢ **Use Password** to create a password for secret mode
  - ➢ **Fingerprint** to unlock secret mode
  - ➢ **Reset Secret Mode** to clear all data in this mode and restore settings to default.

Chapter 17: Camera App

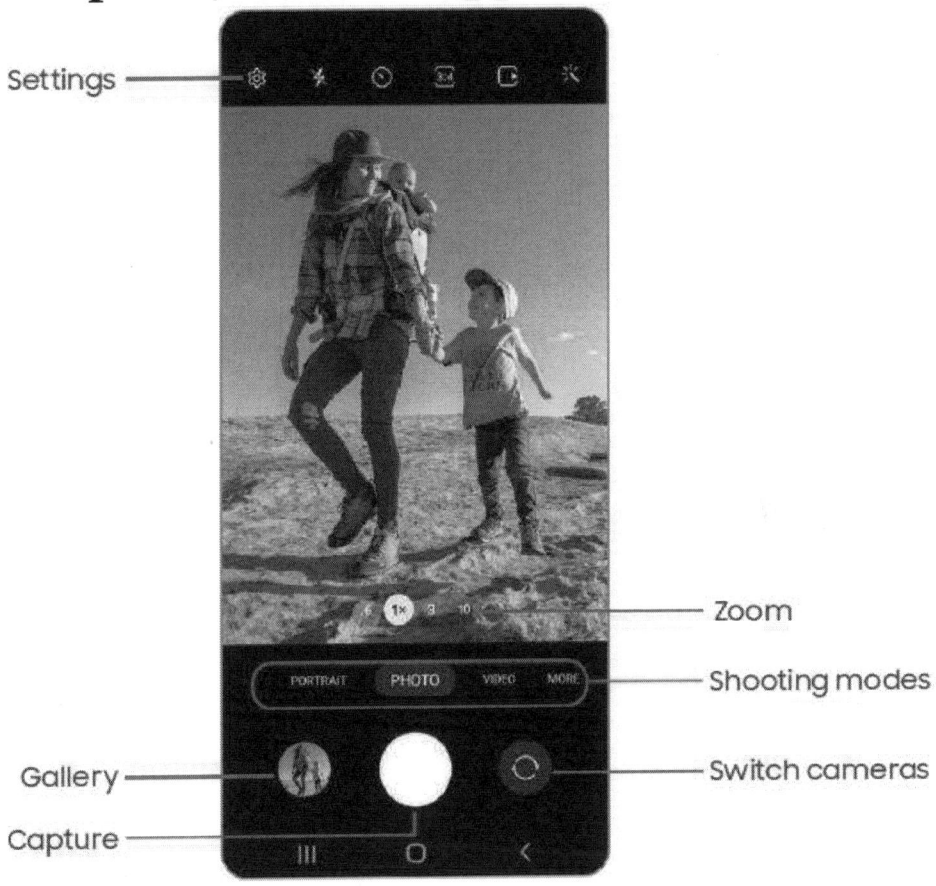

Navigate the Camera Screen

Enjoy beautiful pictures with the rear and front cameras of the S22.

- Open the ◉ camera app.
- Click the image on the camera preview screen where you want your camera to focus.

- Drag the brightness slider right or left to set the brightness.
- Swipe the app screen down or up to switch between the front and back cameras.
- Swipe the screen left and right to view different shooting modes and select one.
- Click ⚙ to customize camera settings
- Press ◯ to take the photo.

Space Zoom
Capture distant photos and still achieve accuracy and clarity.

- Select **Zoom Shortcut** in the camera app to choose your preferred magnification setting.
- Press ◯ to take the photo.

Set Shooting Mode
The S22 Camera has several shooting modes to achieve different functions. To choose a mode.

- Move right & left on the camera screen to view different shooting modes and select one.
- To add more shooting mode, swipe right to the end, click **More,** press ⊕ and then drag desired modes to the shooting modes tray close to the end of the app screen.
- Click **Save** once done and return to the app's home screen.

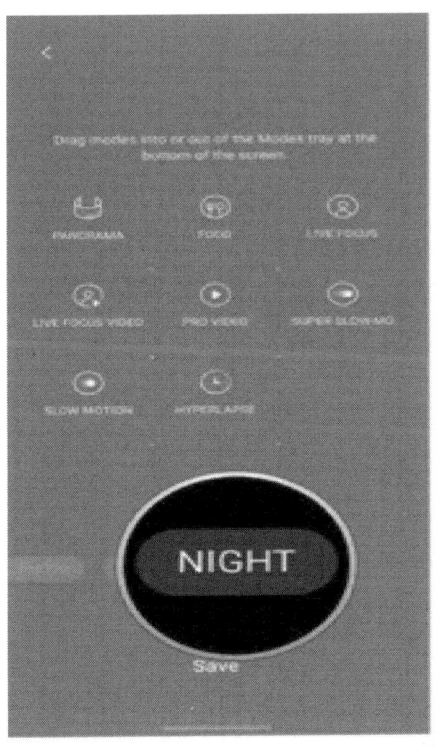 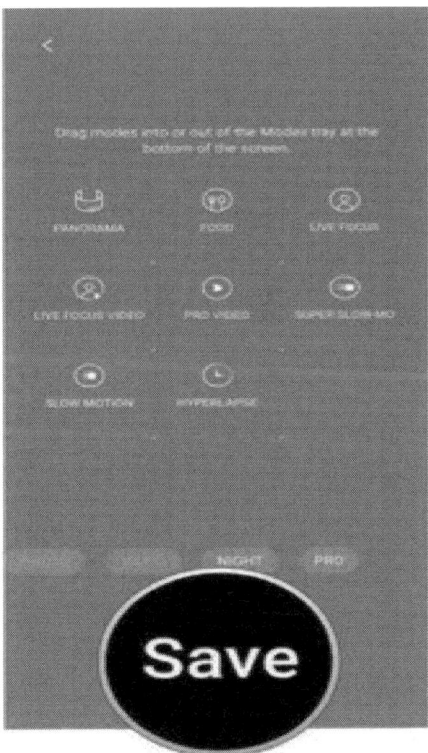

Record Videos
Use your S22 as your professional camera

- Open the Camera app and swipe to the Video shooting mode.

- Click ● to record your video, ◉ to take a picture during the recording, ⏸ to pause the recording, ● to resume, and ■ to stop recording.

Zoom-in Mic
Reduce background noise and increase the volume of the sound recording. This feature can only be used with the Video shooting mode and with the back camera alone.

- Click ⚙ at the top of the camera app screen.
- Click **Advanced Recording Options,** select **Zoom-in Mic,** and tap ⬤ to enable.
- Press ‹ **Back** to go to the app's home screen

- Swipe to the Video shooting mode and press ⏺ to start recording.

- Use your two fingers to zoom out or in on the audio source. You will see the microphone icon showing the changes to the amplification level.

Scene Optimization

This setting adjusts the background colors on your pictures to match the color of the subject.

- Click ⚙ at the top of the camera app screen.

- Then turn on the **Scene Optimizer** switch.

Shot Suggestions

Receive on-screen guides to help you shoot amazing photos

- Click ⚙ at the top of the camera app screen.

- Then turn on the **Shot Suggestions** switch.

Scan QR Codes

Use your device camera to scan QR codes and visit the merchants' sites. Once turned on, the device will automatically detect QR codes

- Click ⚙ at the top of the camera app screen.
- Then turn on the **Scan QR Code** switch.

Swipe Shutter Button

When you swipe the shutter button to the closest edge, you either create a GIF or take burst shots. To activate,

- Click ⚙ at the top of the camera app screen.
- Click **Swipe Shutter Button to** and select an option.

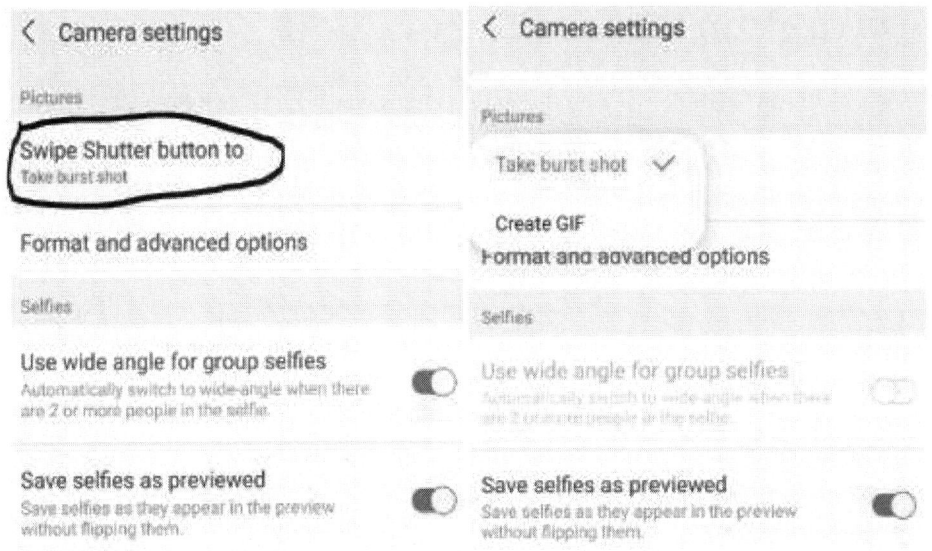

Selfie Settings

See the steps below to customize selfie settings

- Click ⚙ at the top of the camera app screen.
- Toggle on **Save Selfies as Previewed** to save your selfies without flipping them.
- Click **Selfie Color Tone** to choose either a Bright or Natural color for your selfies.

Choose Picture Formats

Choose the formats for your images and other saving options.

- Click ⚙ at the top of the camera app screen.

- Click on **Picture Format.**
- Turn on **High Efficiency Pictures** to save your photos as high efficiency images. This will help to save storage space.
- Turn on **RAW Copies** to have both RAW and JPEG copies of photos captured in Pro Mode.

Video Settings
- Click ⚙ at the top of the camera app screen.
- Toggle on **Auto FPS** to automatically improve light conditions when shooting videos in low-light conditions.
- Toggle on **Video Stabilization** to help your hand stay steady while moving your camera.

Advanced Video Recording Options
- Click ⚙ at the top of the camera app screen and click **Advanced Recording Options**
- Toggle on **Reduce File Size** to use HEVC format for recording videos. This will save space on your device.

- Toggle on **HDR10+ Videos** to record your videos in HDR10+.

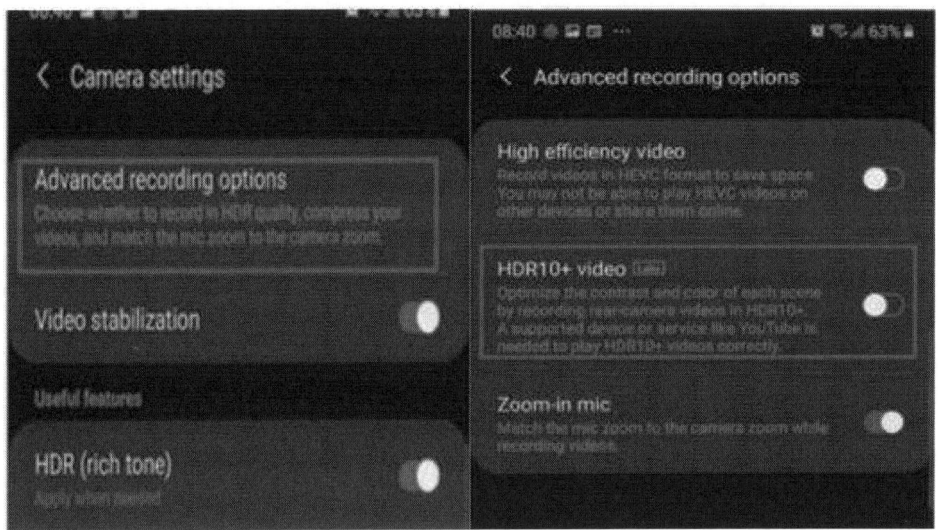

General Camera Setting

- Click ⚙ at the top of the camera app screen and scroll down to **General.**
- Toggle on **Auto HDR** to get in more detail in the dark and light areas of your shot.
- Toggle on **Tracking Auto-Focus** to focus the rear camera on the subject even when they move.
- Toggle on **Grid Lines** to see the viewfinder grid lines when shooting a video or taking a

photo. This setting helps compose your video or photo.

- Toggle on **Location Tags** to include GPS location tags in your media content.
- Toggle on **Shutter Sounds** to play a sound when shooting photos.
- Toggle on **Vibration Feedback** to feel vibrations when you tap the camera app screen.

Shooting Methods
Use this option to customize your shooting modes and methods.

- Click ⚙ at the top of the camera app screen and scroll down to **General.**
- Click **Shooting Methods.**
- Click '**Press Volume Keys to**' to assign a function to the volume keys if you press them while the camera app is open.

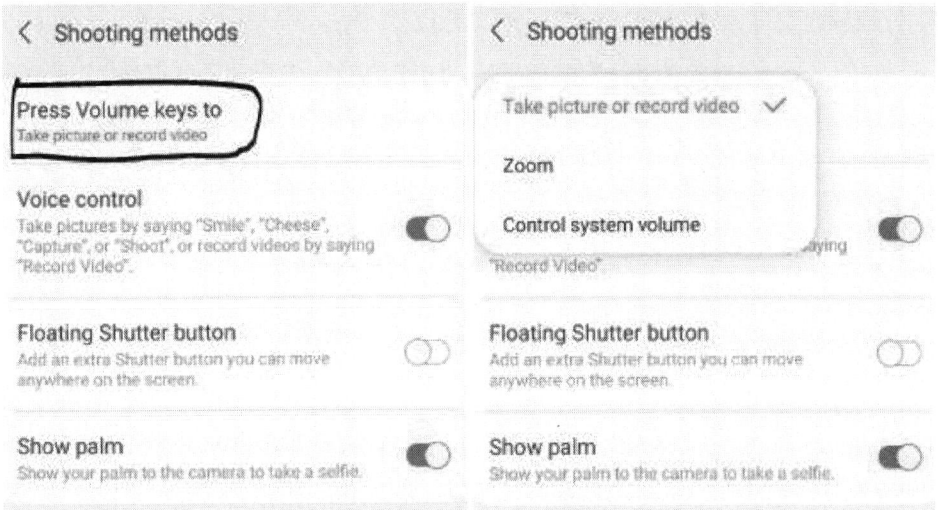

- Toggle on **Voice Commands** to control your camera with your voice.

- Toggle on **Floating Shutter Button** to include an additional shutter button that you can move around the camera screen.

- Toggle on **Show Palm** to face your palm towards the camera and have your picture taken automatically.

- Click **Reset Settings** to return the camera setting to default.

Camera Settings to Keep

After making changes to the camera setting, you can store the settings to use them over and again.

- Click ⚙ at the top of the camera app screen.
- Scroll down to **General** and click on **Settings to Keep.**
- Toggle on **Camera Mode** to save the last shooting mode you used.
- Toggle on **Selfie Angle** to save the last angle you used for selfies.
- Toggle on **Filters** to save your filter settings
- Toggle on **Super Steady** to have the mode constantly on even after restarting the app.

Chapter 18: Clock App

Set alarms and track time in the Clock app.

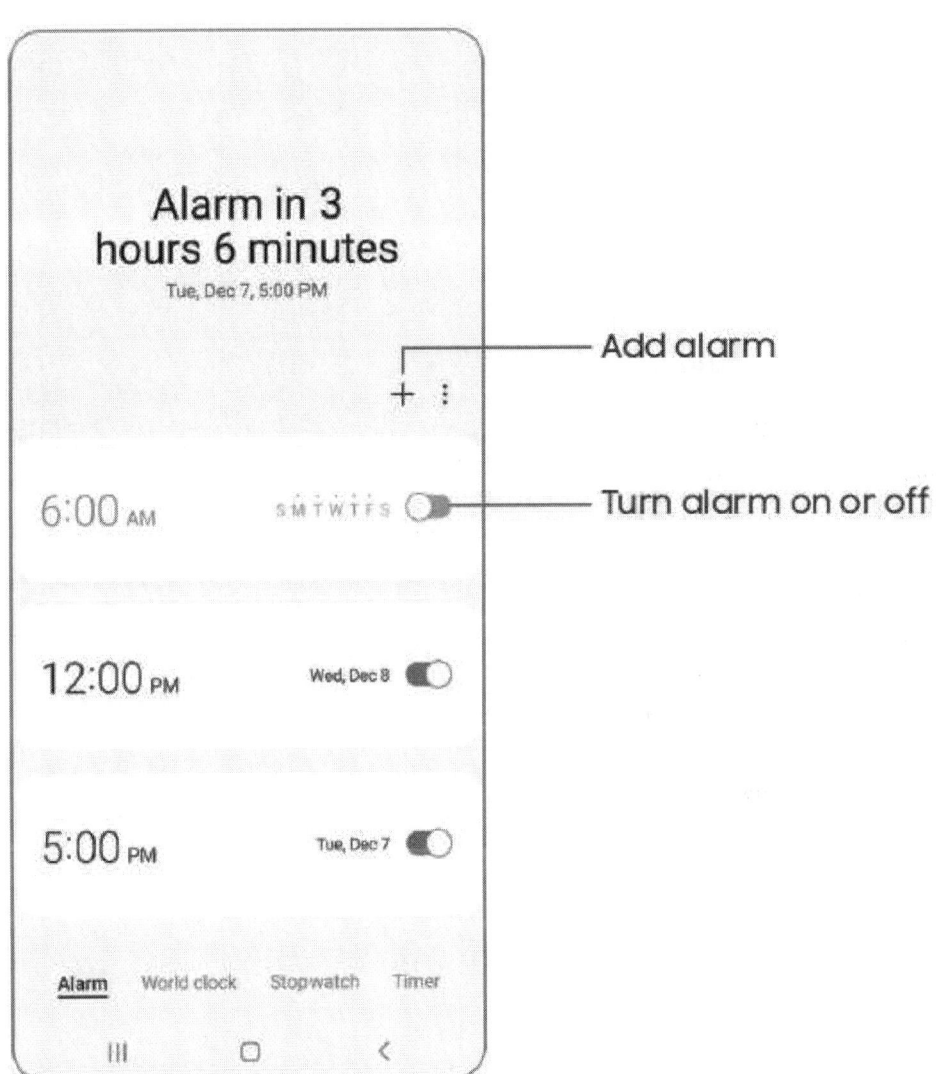

Set Alarms

You can choose to have the alarm repeat continuously or just for one time.

- Click **Alarm** at the bottom of the app and press ✛.
- Name the alarm, choose the day, and set the time.
- To choose a sound for the alarm, tap **Alarm Sound,** turn on the switch, and make your selection.
- To use vibration, tap **Vibration,** turn on the ⬤ switch, and make your selection.
- To see the option to snooze the alarm, press **Snooze,** turn on the ⬤ switch and make your selection.
- Click **Save** to finish.

Set Your Sleep and Wake Time
Set a bedtime reminder and put your phone in Bedtime mode once it gets to the set time.

- Click **Alarm** at the bottom of the app and press ⋮.

155

- Click **Set Bedtime and Wake-up Time** and press **Next**
- Use the circle on your screen to set your sleep time, then press **Next**
- Turn on **Bedtime Mode** and click **Reminder Notification.**
- Click **Next,** make other changes, and press **Done.**

Delete an Alarm
- Touch and hold the alarm you want to delete, then press **Delete.**

Alert Settings
Configure your phone to vibrate for timers & alarms even when sound mode is on Vibrate or Mute.

- Press ⋮ in the app and select **Settings.**
- Turn on the **Vibrate for Alarms and Timers** switch

World Clock
Track current time in different cities of the world.

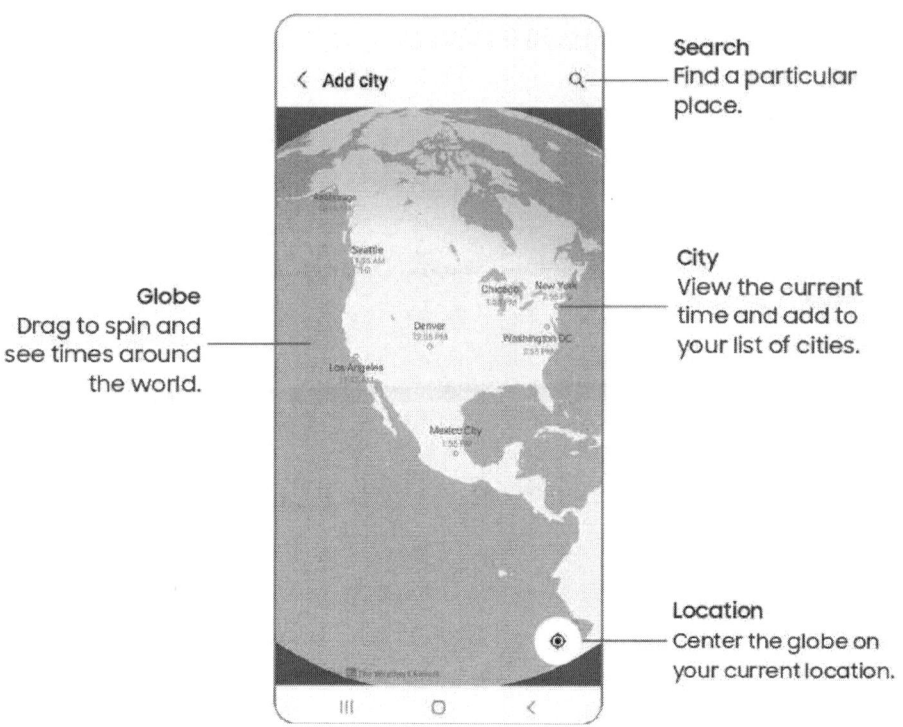

- Click **World Clock** at the bottom of the app and press ✚.
- Move the map to get to a city you want, or use the search button at the top to search for the select.
- Tap the city and press **Add.**
- To delete the city, go to the World Clock screen, press and hold the city, then tap 🗑 **Delete.**

157

Time Zone Converter
Set the time in one city and see corresponding time in other cities of the world

- Click **World Clock** at the bottom of the app and press ⋮.

- Click **Time Zone Converter** and click ▼ to set another city or press ✛ to add a new city that is not on the list.

- In the time screen, select the time you want to view, and you will see the corresponding time for the other cities in the list. For example, set 5:00PM in New York and see what time it would be in Vancouver, Florida, and other cities of your choice.

- Tap **Reset** to change to the current time.

Weather Settings
- Click **World Clock** at the bottom of the app and press ⋮.

- Click **Settings** and turn on the **Show Weather** switch.
- Click **Temperature** to select Celsius or Fahrenheit.

Stopwatch
Time events using the stopwatch.

- Click **Stopwatch** at the bottom of the app and press **Start**.
- Press **Start** to begin and **Stop** to end.
- Press **Pause** to stop temporarily and **Resume** to continue.

Preset Time
Save and name preset timers

- Click **Timer** at the bottom of the app and press ✛.
- Name the timer, set countdown time, and click **Add**.

- To edit preset timers, press ⋮ and select **Edit Preset Timers.**

Timer Options
Customize the timer

- Click **Timer**, press ⋮ and click **Settings.**
- Scroll to **Timer** and turn on the desired switches.

Chapter 19: Gallery App

Your media content is stored in the Gallery app on your device.

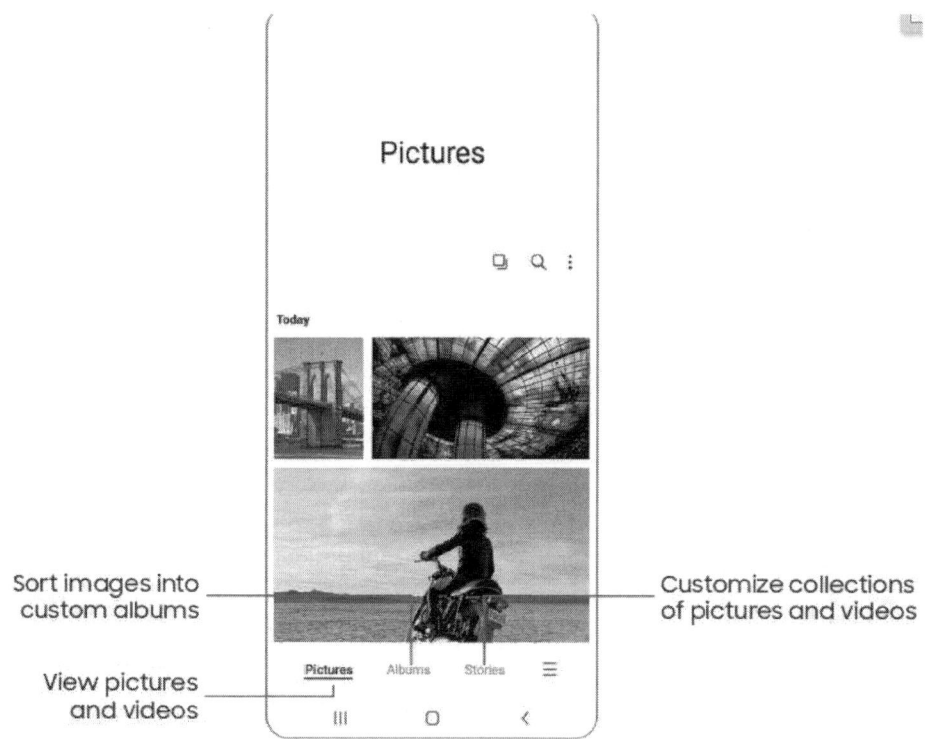

- Click the ✷ icon in the app or home screen to open the Gallery app.

View Pictures

- Open the Gallery app and click **Pictures.** Swipe either way to view media content

- Select a picture to expand it, tap ♡ to add it to your Favorites.
- Tap ⋮ at the bottom of the image to view more options for that photo:
    - ➢ Click **Set as Wallpaper** to use the image as your wallpaper
    - ➢ Click **Details** to see time, date, and other details
    - ➢ Click **Remaster Picture** to automatically improve the image.
    - ➢ Click **Add Portrait Effect** to reduce or improve the background visibility in your portrait photos.
    - ➢ Select **Copy to Clipboard** to paste the image in a different app
    - ➢ Click **Move to Secure Folder** to transfer the photo to a secure folder
    - ➢ Select **Print** to print the image.

Edit Photos

The gallery tool has several editing tools for your photos.

- Open the photo you want to edit and press .
- Click ※ to improve the appearance of the photo.
- Click ⟳ to crop, rotate, flip, or make other changes to the photo.
- Click ⊗ for filter and color effects
- Click ☼ to change the photo's brightness, contract, exposure, etc.
- Click ☺ to add stickers, text, and handwriting on the photo.
- Click ⋮ to see more options for that photo.
- Click **Revert** to discard all editing on the photo.
- Then tap **Save** to complete.

Play Video
- Click the **Pictures** tab in the Gallery app and press a video to open it. Tap ♡ to add it to your Favorites.

- Tap ⋮ at the bottom of the video to view more options:
  - ➤ Click **Set as Wallpaper** to use the video as your wallpaper on the Lock Screen.
  - ➤ Click **Details** to see time, date, and other details
  - ➤ Click **Move to Secure Folder** to transfer the video to a secure folder
  - ➤ Click **Open in Video Player** to play the video in the default video player.

- Tap ▶ to play the open video.

Video Brightness
Improve the quality of your videos.

- Go to the Settings app and select **Advanced Features.**

- Click **Video Brightness** and choose one option.

Edit Video

- Open the video you want to edit and press ✏️.

- Click 🔊 to add background music to your video and control the volume levels.

- Click ▶ to play the edited video.

- Click ✂ to cut portions of the videos.

- Click ⬜ to crop, rotate, flip, or make other changes to the video.

- Click ◉ for filter and color effects

- Click ☼ to change the photo's brightness, contract, exposure, etc.

- Click ☺ to add stickers, text, and handwriting on the photo.

- Click ⋮ to see more options for that photo.

165

- Click **Revert** to discard all editing on the photo.
- Then tap **Save** and confirm the changes.

Share Videos and Pictures

- Click the **Pictures** tab in the Gallery app and tap ⋮ at the bottom
- Click **Edit,** select all the media you want, and click **Share.**
- Follow the prompts to complete

Delete Media Contents

- Click the **Pictures** tab in the Gallery app and tap ⋮ at the bottom
- Click **Edit,** select all the media you want, and click **Delete.** Confirm action once prompted.

Group Similar Images

- At the top of the Gallery home screen, select ▣ to **Group Similar Images.** Tap ▣ to ungroup.

Chapter 20: My Files

Find and manage files on your S22, including sound clips, documents, audio, and videos.

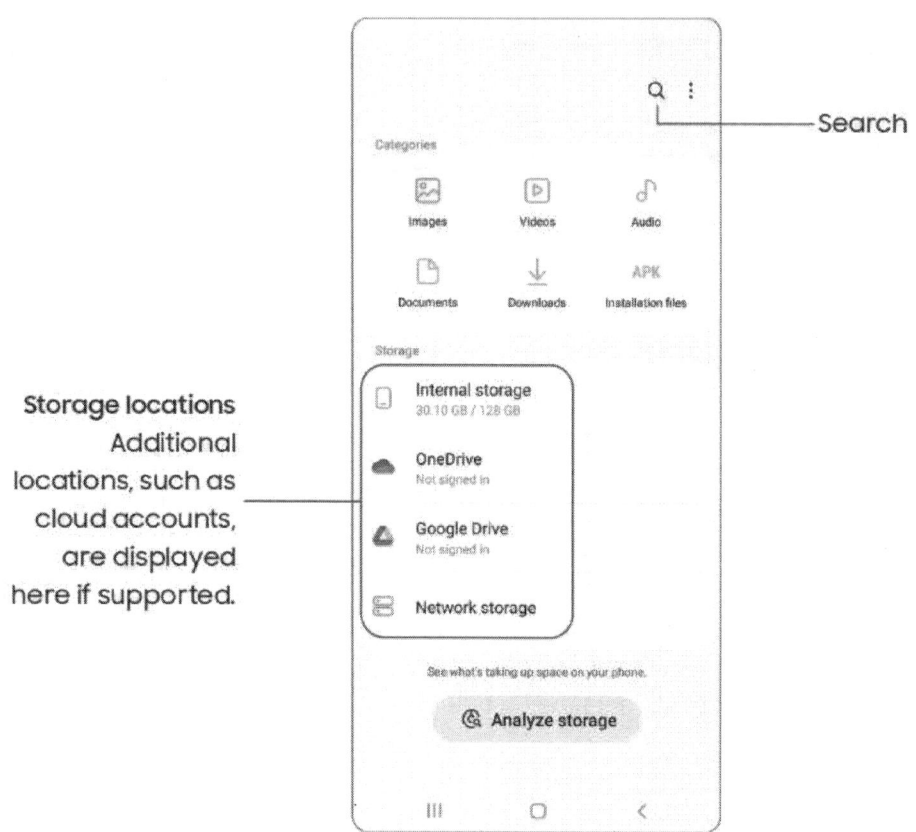

Storage locations
Additional locations, such as cloud accounts, are displayed here if supported.

Search

File Groups

Open the Files app to see different categories

- Click **Recent Files** to see documents that you viewed or added recently.

- Scroll down to **Categories** to find different groups for the content on your device. Click on a group to access the document it contains.
- Click **Storage** to view all the files saved on your device.
- Click **Analyze Storage** at the bottom of the screen to see the items using the most space in your storage. Click on each category to view the items in it and delete the files you no longer need.

Trash Folder

Files you delete would stay in the trash folder for another 30 days before it gets deleted permanently from your device. If you erroneously delete a file, you will find it in the trash folder. See the steps below to find this folder:

- Open ⊙ **My Files** app, tap ⋮ and click **Trash.**

- Select the item you want to restore and click **Restore** or click **Delete** to permanently delete it.

Follow the steps below to turn on the trash folder:

- Open ⊙**My Files** app, tap ⋮ and click **Settings.**
- Then turn on the **Trash** button to keep deleted items for 30 days.

Delete Items from My File
You can delete items right on the My File app

- Open the app and click the category that has the item you want to delete
- Press down on the item until you see the checkmark, click **Delete** and then click **Move to Trash.**

Large File Size Settings
Use this setting to choose how big a file needs to be for it to be flagged when you analyze storage.

- Open ⬤**My Files** app, tap ⋮ and click **Settings**.
- Click **Large File Size** and choose from the sizes listed on your screen or click **Custom Size** to enter a different size.

Chapter 21: Samsung Pay

Add your bank cards to your S22 and make payments with your device at any time.

Set Up Samsung Pay

- Open the Samsung Pay app and allow the app access to your phone calls.
- Click **Get Started** and enter your Samsung account password to verify it's you.
- Read and agree to the app's terms and conditions to continue.
- Choose a verification method for the app or skip to continue using your default security method.

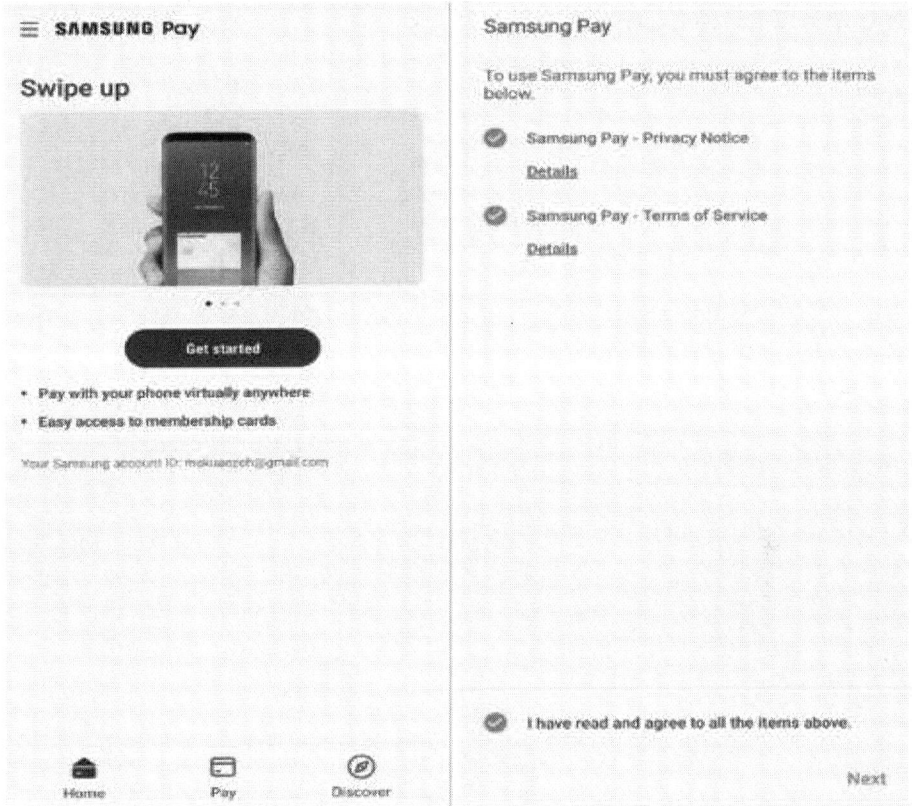

- Then click **Add Card** to enter your card details or click **Later** to add the card in the future.
- To add the bank card in the future, open the app and click **Payment Cards.** You may also click **Memberships** to add membership cards from eligible businesses.

Use Samsung Pay
To pay using the Samsung Pay app,

- Open the app and select a card to pay with.
- Authorize the transaction with your selected authorization method, then place your phone close to the store's card reader.
- Samsung will send you a receipt to your registered email once the payment goes through.

Quick Access
Quick access allows you to use the Samsung Pay app from the home screen, lock screen, or screen off. To turn it off,

- Open Samsung Pay and click ≡.
- Select ⚙ **Settings** at the top and click **Quick Access**
- Then turn on the ⬤ switch for each of the options.

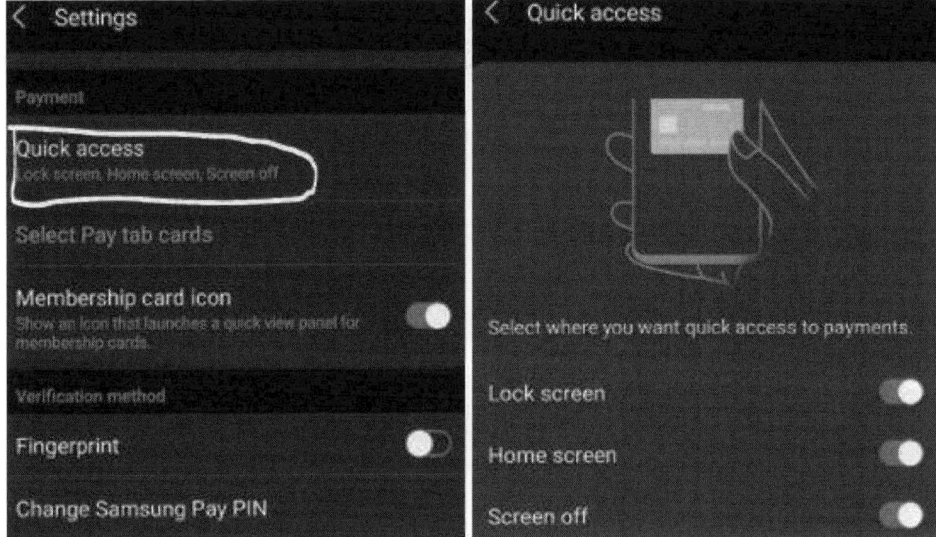

To use quick access:

- Swipe upward from the end of any of the screen to show your Samsung Pay payment card.
- Swipe down on the card to close the feature.

Chapter 22: Samsung Notes

Create notes on your Samsung S22. Add images, music, voice recordings, and more, also share notes with your social networks.

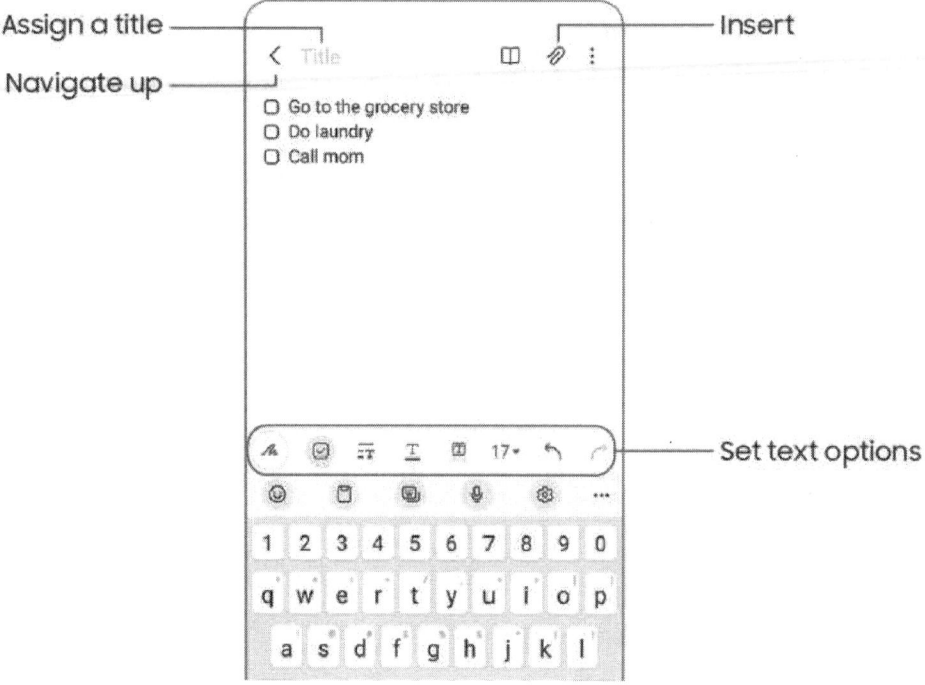

Create New Notes

- Open the ⬛ Samsung Notes app and click ✎ to start a new note.
- Title your note if desired and enter desired content.

Voice Recordings

Create notes while recording an audio. Perfect for meetings or lectures.

- Click ✏️ to start a new note, then click 📎 and select **Voice Recording.**
- Create your text content while the audio recording is on.

Edit Notes

- Click a note to open it, click ✏️ and make your changes.
- Click ‹ to save and click again to return to the app's home screen.

Open PDFs in Samsung Note

You can import PDFs into the Notes app.

- Click 📄+ in the app's home screen and select the PDF you want to open.

Search Notes

- Click 🔍 in the app's home screen to search for a keyword

Sort Notes
Change the arrangement of notes in the app

- Click ⋮ in the app's home screen and tap **Sort.**
- Then choose a style of your choice. Click **Done** to finish
- Toggle on **Pin Favorites to Top** to keep your favorite notes at the top of the app's home page.

Delete, Share, Move Notes

- Click ⋮ in the app's home screen, then click **Edit.**
- Select the notes you want and then choose an option at the bottom of your screen

Change Page View
Choose to see your notes as a list, simple list, or grid

- Click ⋮ in the app's home screen, click **View,** and choose the appearance of your choice.

View Trash Folder

Notes you delete will remain in the trash folder for up to 15 days. To view the trash folder,

- Click ≡ in the app's main page and select **Trash.**

Chapter 23: Accounts

Add and manage your accounts

Add a Google Account

Access your Google account in the Galaxy S22, including your Gmail and Google cloud storage.

- Open Settings and click **Accounts and Backup.**
- Click **Manage Accounts** and click ➕**Add Account.**
- Select **Google** and follow the prompts to add your Google account.

Add a Samsung Account

Sign in or create a Samsung account to use Samsung apps and access exclusive Samsung items.

- Open Settings and click **Samsung Account.**
- Agree to the terms, if any.
- Enter your Samsung account details/ create a new one.

Add an Outlook Account
Manage your Outlook emails on the S22 device

- Open Settings and click **Accounts and Backup.**
- Click **Manage Accounts** and click ➕**Add Account.**
- Select **Outlook** and follow the prompts to add your Outlook account.

Account Settings
Individual accounts have their own settings, but you can also modify common settings for all active accounts.

- Open Settings and click **Accounts and Backup.**
- Click **Manage Accounts** and click an account to change its settings.

Remove an Account
To delete an account from your Galaxy,

- Open Settings and click **Accounts and Backup.**
- Click **Manage Accounts,** select the account, and click **Remove Account.**

Chapter 24: Connections

Connect to a Wi-Fi Network
- Open **Settings** and click **Connections.**
- Select **Wi-Fi** and tap ⬤ to turn it on and search for networks.
- Click a network, enter the password, and press **Connect.**

Manage Saved Networks
See all your saved networks and delete the ones you no longer want

- Open **Settings** and click **Connections.**
- Select **Wi-Fi**, click ⋮ and tap **Advanced**
- Click **Manage Networks** to see saved networks. Click a network and turn on/off **Auto Reconnect** or click **Forget** to delete the network.

Advanced Wi-Fi Settings
- Open **Settings** and click **Connections.**

- Select **Wi-Fi**, click ⋮ and tap **Advanced** for the following options:

  ➢ Turn on **Switch to Mobile Data** ⬤ to use mobile data when the Wi-Fi connection is weak or unavailable.

  ➢ Turn on **Turn on Wi-Fi Automatically** ⬤ to connect to Wi-Fi in places you use frequently.

  ➢ Turn on **Sync with Samsung Cloud** ⬤ to sync all Wi-Fi profiles with your Samsung account

  ➢ Turn on **Detect Suspicious Network** ⬤ to receive notifications whenever the device detects suspicious activities on your current network.

  ➢ Turn on **Show Network Quality Info** ⬤ to view information like network stability and speed in the list of Wi-Fi networks.

> Turn on **Wi-Fi Power Saving Mode** to analyze wi-fi traffic patterns to save battery usage.

> Turn on **Show Wi-Fi Pop-up** to receive notifications of available Wi-Fi network when opening apps

> Turn on **Hotspot 2.0** to automatically connect your device to Wi-Fi networks that support the Hotspot 2.0.

Wi-Fi Control History

View a list of apps that recently turned your Wi-Fi off or on.

- Open **Settings** and click **Connections**.
- Select **Wi-Fi**, click and tap **Advanced**
- Click **Wi-Fi Control History** to see the list.

Wi-Fi Direct

Share data between multiple devices using Wi-Fi.

- Open **Settings** and click **Connections.**
- Select **Wi-Fi** and turn it ⬤ on.
- Click ⋮ , tap **Wi-Fi Direct.**
- Select a device and follow the on-screen prompts to connect

Disconnect from Wi-Fi Direct

- Open **Settings** and click **Connections.**
- Select **Wi-Fi**, click ⋮ , and tap **Wi-Fi Direct.**
- Then tap a connected device to disconnect it

Connect to Bluetooth
Pair your S22 with other Bluetooth-enabled devices like your headphones and car system.

- Open **Settings** and click **Connections.**
- Select **Bluetooth** and turn it on.
- Select a device and follow the on-screen guide to connect.

Rename Paired Bluetooth Device

This would make it easy for you to recognize the device

- Open **Settings** and click **Connections.**
- Select **Bluetooth** and turn it on.
- Tap ⚙ beside the device name and press **Rename.**
- Choose a new name and press **Rename.**

Unpair From a Bluetooth Device

Once you unpair, the device will no longer automatically recognize the other device, and you would need to pair them again.

- Open **Settings** and click **Connections.**
- Select **Bluetooth** and turn it on.
- Tap ⚙ beside the device name and press **Unpair.**
- Press **Unpair** again to finish.

Change your Phone's Bluetooth Name
- Open **Settings** and click **Connections.**

- Select **Bluetooth**, click ⋮ and tap **Advanced**.
- Click **Phone Name** and enter the new name.

Advanced Options
Find below additional Bluetooth settings.

- Open **Settings** and click **Connections.**
- Select **Bluetooth**, click ⋮ and tap **Advanced**.
- Turn on **Sync with Samsung Cloud** to sync all Bluetooth-transferred files with your Samsung account
- Click **Received Files** to view the items received via Bluetooth
- Click **Ringtone Sync** to use your device ringtone for calls received through connected Bluetooth devices.
- Click **Block Pairing Requests** to block selected devices from sending your pairing requests.

Bluetooth Control History
View a list of apps that recently used Bluetooth.

- Open **Settings** and click **Connections.**

- Select **Bluetooth**, click ⋮ and tap **Advanced**
- Click **Bluetooth Control History** to see the list.

Bluetooth Scan History

View the list of apps that recently scanned for nearby Bluetooth devices and manage the Bluetooth access for apps.

- Open **Settings** and click **Connections.**
- Select **Bluetooth**, click ⋮ , tap **Advanced** and click **Bluetooth Scan History**

Airplane Mode

Airplane mode would automatically turn off calls, text, Wi-Fi, Bluetooth, and mobile data. However, you can turn on Bluetooth and Wi-Fi again in the Quick Settings panel or Settings app. To turn on Airplane mode,

- Open **Settings** and click **Connections.**
- Select **Airplane Mode** and turn it on.

Mobile Networks
Configure mobile network settings

- Open **Settings,** click **Connections** and click **Mobile Networks** to configure settings, including Mobile Data, Allow 2G Service, Data Roaming, and Access Point Names.

Check Data Usage
See how much data your device has used for both Wi-Fi and mobile network.

- Open **Settings,** click **Connections,** and click **Data Usage**

Turn on Data Saver
Prevent specified apps from receiving or sending data in the background.

- Open **Settings** and click **Connections.**
- Click **Data Usage,** tap **Data Saver,** and turn it on.
- To permit certain apps to have unlimited data usage, click "**Allowed to use data while**

Data saver is on" and toggle on apps that should have this setting.

Mobile Hotspot

Use your phone data as a Wi-fi network for other devices. To turn on Hotspot,

- Open **Settings** and click **Connections.**
- Click **Mobile Hotspot and Tethering** and turn it on.
- Turn on Wi-fi on the other device and search for your device under the Wi-Fi list.
- Then enter your hotspot password to complete.

Auto Hotspot

Automatically share a hotspot connection with devices that have the same Samsung account login details.

- Open **Settings** and click **Connections.**
- Click **Mobile Hotspot and Tethering** and turn on ⬤**Auto Hotspot.**

Nearby Device Scanning

Connect to other devices using the Nearby Device feature. You will receive notifications whenever there is a device to connect to. You can use this feature to share content between both devices.

- Open **Settings** and click **Connections.**
- Click **More connection settings,** tap **Nearby device scanning** and turn it on .

Connect to a Printer

Your printer would need to be on the same Wi-Fi network as your S22.

- Open **Settings** and click **Connections.**
- Click **More connection settings** and tap **Printing.**
- Select **Default Print Service,** tap and click **Add Printer.**
- For printers that require a plugin, click **Download Plugin** and use the on-screen prompts to add a printing service.

Chapter 25: Notification

Notification Pop-Up Style

Customize the way you want notifications to pop up on your screen

- Open **Settings,** click **Notifications,** and select a pop-up style:
  - ➢ **Brief:** the notification will flash on your screen and then disappear. Click **Included Apps** to select apps that should use this notification style. Click **Brief Pop-up Settings** to turn on **Show Even While Screen is Off.** This setting will send you notifications even when your device is in sleep mode. You can also customize other settings on this screen.

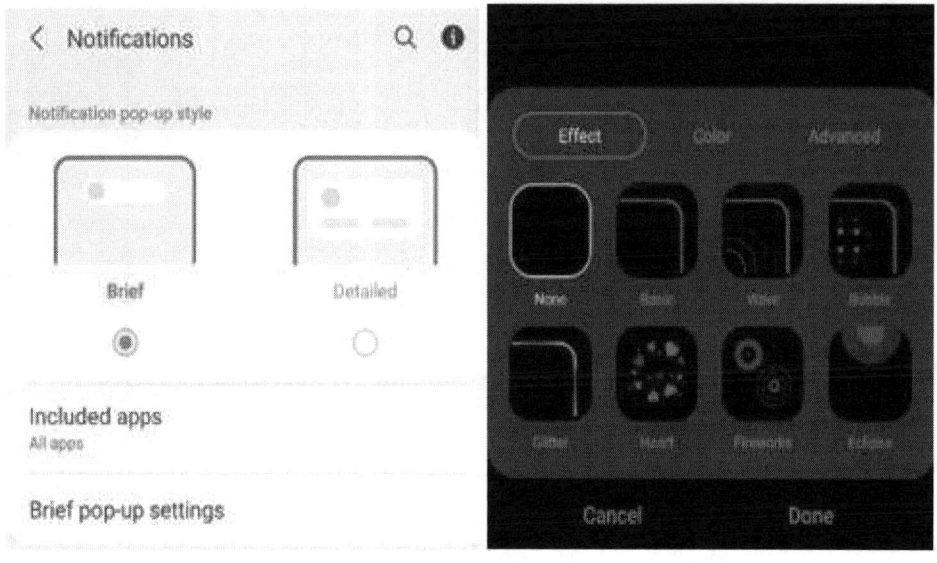

> **Detailed:** choose this to see a preview of the content of the notification

Recently Sent Notifications

See a list of apps that recently sent you notifications:

- Open **Settings** and click **Notifications.**
- You will find recently received notifications under **Recently Sent.** Click **More** for a complete list.
- Click on individual apps to modify the notification setting for that app.

Do Not Disturb

Use this setting to block notifications and sounds for a period. You have the option of excluding certain apps, people, and alarms from the block. To turn on,

- Open **Settings,** click **Notifications,** and click **Do not Disturb.**

- Turn on the **Do Not Disturb** switch to use it now, & click **For How Long** to set a period for the feature to be active.

- You can also customize the feature to come on at a scheduled time. To set up DND for the period you're asleep, click **Sleeping** and set up the days and times. Or click **Add Schedule** to set up DND for times outside your sleeping hours. These settings will automatically place your device on DND within the specified times.

- To make exceptions for certain people, scroll to **Exceptions,** click **Calls, Messages, and**

Conversations, and make the necessary settings for **Calls, Messages,** and **Conversations**. You may turn on the **Repeat Callers** button to allow calls from numbers that have tried to reach you multiple times in that period.

- To make exceptions for alarms and sounds, click **Alarms and Sounds** and turn on the desired options.

- To make an exception for certain apps, click **Apps,** and tap **Add Apps** to select the apps.

Hide Notifications
You can also choose not to receive any notifications on your phone.

- Open **Settings,** click **Notifications,** and click **Hide Notifications.**

- Turn on the **Hide All** switch to block notifications from any app or turn on any other switch as it suits your needs.

Show Notification Icons

Choose the number of notifications that should appear on the status bar per time.

- Open **Settings,** click **Notifications,** and click **Advanced settings.**

- Click **Show Notification Icons** and choose a count.

Show Battery Percentage

See your battery percentage on the top of your screen, also called the status bar

- Open **Settings,** click **Notifications,** and click **Advanced settings.**

- Then turn on the **Show Battery Percentage** ⬤ switch.

View Notification History

Turn on this option to view snoozed and recent notifications

- Open **Settings,** click **Notifications,** and click **Advanced settings.**

- Click **Notification History** and turn on the ⬜ switch.

Floating Notifications

The notification will float on your screen while using other apps. To turn on,

- Open **Settings,** click **Notifications,** and click **Advanced settings.**
- Click **Floating Notifications** and choose either **Smart Pop-up View** or **Bubbles. Smart Pop-up View** notification will appear like the Facebook messenger notification at the top of your screen, allowing you to use other apps simultaneously. The bubbles option will float on your screen in bubbles.

Notification Reminders

Receive reminders to check pending notifications from select services and apps. You would need to clear notifications to stop receiving the reminders.

- Open **Settings,** click **Notifications,** and click **Advanced settings.**
- Click **Notification Reminders,** turn on the switch, and customize the settings to suit your needs.

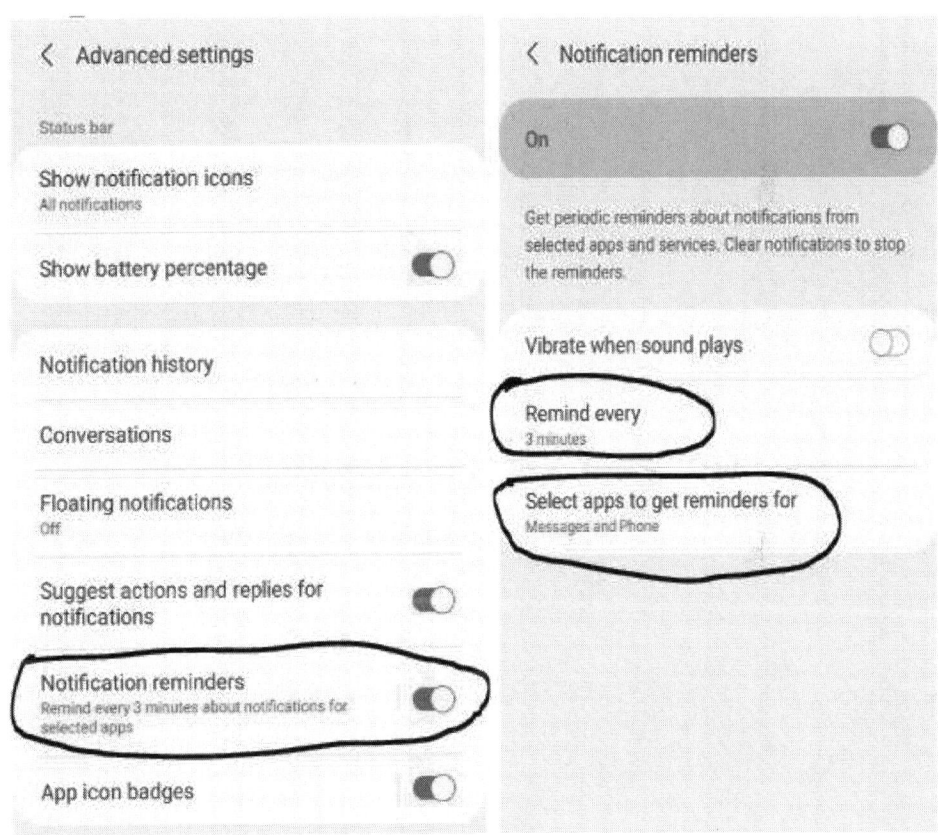

Advanced Notification Settings
Here are other settings you can apply for your notifications

- Open **Settings,** click **Notifications,** and click **Advanced settings.**

- Toggle on **'Suggest Actions and Replies for Notifications'** switch to receive suggestions on what to do with notification items.

- Toggle on **'App Icon Badges'** to see badges on apps that have unread notifications

- Click **Conversations** to see conversation notifications. Tap a conversation notification to customize notification settings for that conversation.

- Turn on **Show Snooze Button** to get a button to use for snoozing notifications.

- Click **Wireless Emergency Alerts** to modify the emergency alert notification.

Chapter 26: Sounds and Vibrations

Sound Mode

Place your phone ringing on mute, vibrate or sound in two ways:

1. Use the volume keys to place the phone or mute, vibrate, or sound.

Or follow the settings below:

- Open **Settings** and click **Sounds and Vibration.**
- Select an option under **Sound Mode: Sound, Mute,** or **Vibrate**
  - ➢ If you select **Sound**, you may turn on the **Vibrate While Ringing** button to have your phone vibrate when you have an incoming call.
  - ➢ For the Mute option, you can choose a period to keep the phone muted. For this,

toggle on **Temporary Mute,** click **Mute For,** and choose an option.

Vibration
Control when and how your S22 vibrates

- Open **Settings,** click **Sounds and Vibration,** and select **Vibrate** under **Sound Mode.**
- Click **Call Vibration Pattern** to select a vibration pattern for calls.
- Click **Notification Vibration Pattern** to select a vibration pattern for new notifications.
- Click **Vibration Intensity** and use the slider to select the vibration intensity level for different options.

Device Volume
Set volume levels for media, system, ringtones, and notification sounds.

- Open **Settings,** click **Sounds and Vibration,** and select **Volume.**
- Then use the slider to set the sound level for the different options.
- Toggle on **Use Volume Keys for Media** switch to control media volume using your phone's volume keys.

Media Volume Limit
Set a limit for your device volume while using headphones or speakers

- Open **Settings,** click **Sounds and Vibration,** and select **Volume.**
- Click ⋮ and select **Media Volume Limit.**
- Turn on the switch and use the slider under **Custom Volume Limit** to create a limit.
- Turn on **Set Volume Limit PIN** to lock this setting with a PIN so that others would be unable to make changes.

Ringtone

Choose your preferred audio to use as a ringtone.

- Open **Settings,** click **Sounds and Vibration,** and select **Ringtone.**
- Click a ringtone to play it and select it.
- Alternatively, press ✚ to select audio from your media as your ringtone.

Notification Sound

Choose a sound to use for incoming notifications

- Open **Settings,** click **Sounds and Vibration,** and select **Notification Sound.**
- Click a sound to play it and select it.

System Sounds

Choose a sound for system actions like charging, touch interactions, keyboard activity, and more.

- Open **Settings,** click **Sounds and Vibration,** and select **System Sound.**
- Click a sound to play it and select it.

Dolby Atmos

Certain sounds are designed for Atmos. Customize the Dolby Atmos settings to enjoy quality sounds.

- Open **Settings,** click **Sounds and Vibration,** and select **Sound Quality and Effects.**
- Click **Dolby Atmos,** turn on the ⬤ switch, and choose when to use this setting.
- Return to the previous screen and turn on the **Dolby Atmos for Gaming** ⬤ switch to enjoy great sounds while playing games.

Equalizer

The S22 has customized audio presets for different music genres. You can also create one for yourself using the custom option. To do this,

- Open **Settings,** click **Sounds and Vibration,** and select **Sound Quality and Effects.**

- Click **Equalizer** and choose a setting or click **Custom** to create yours.

UHQ Upscaler

This setting improves the quality of sounds you hear when using a headset. You would need to connect a headset to access this setting

- Open **Settings,** click **Sounds and Vibration** and select **Sound Quality and Effects.**
- Click **UHQ Upscaler** and choose an option.

Adapt Sound

You can customize audio sounds based on your age and other preference.

- Open **Settings,** click **Sounds and Vibration,** and select **Sound Quality and Effects.**
- Click **Adapt Sound** and choose the profile that best suits you. Then click ⚙ beside your option to further customize it.

- You can also use **Test My hearing** to allow your S22 to choose the best sound for you.

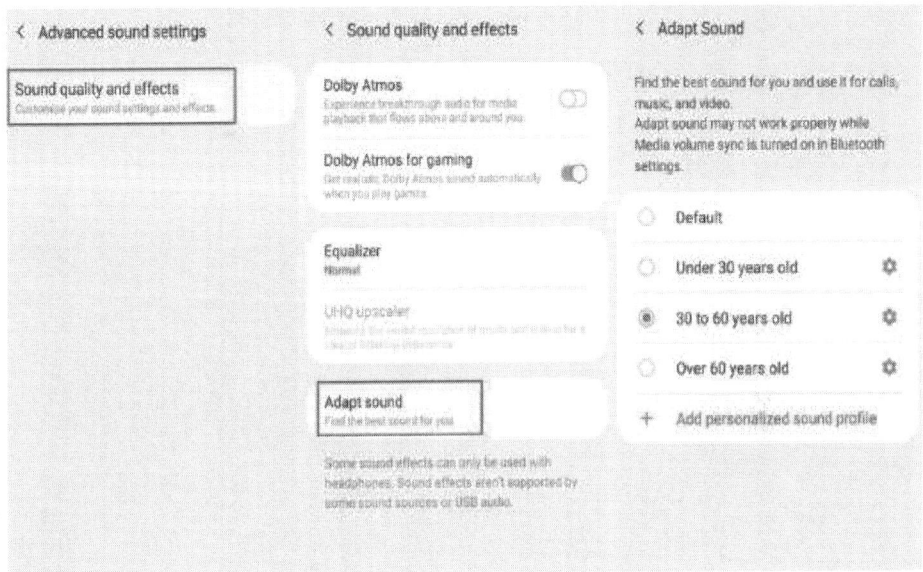

Separate App Sound

You can configure an app to play its media sound on a separate Bluetooth or headset device, different from the one you use for other apps. You would need to connect to your Bluetooth device before doing the steps below:

- Open **Settings,** click **Sounds and Vibration,** and select **Separate App Sound.**

- Activate the **Turn on Now** switch, then click **App** to choose multimedia apps that you want to play its sound on a different audio device.
- Once done, return to the previous screen and click **Audio Device** to select the audio output/ device to use for the apps.

Chapter 27: Display

You can customize font size, screen brightness, resolution, timeout delay, and other display settings.

Easy Mode
Make your texts and icons larger.

- Open **Settings,** click **Display,** and select **Dark.**
- Turn on the ⬤ switch to see the following options:
    - ➢ Click **Touch and Hold Delay** to set the length of time you need to touch the screen for the action to be regarded as touch and hold,
    - ➢ Click **High Contrast Keyboard** to select a keyboard that has high contrast colors.

Show Charging Information
Display current battery level and expected time to get the device fully charged when your screen is off.

- Open **Settings,** click **Display,** and turn on **Show Charging Information.**

Dark Mode

Use a darker theme at night to help your eyes adjust to the lighting condition. You can also use this setting in the daytime if in an environment with poor lighting conditions. It would darken the screen brightness and make the phone screen friendly to your eyes.

- Open **Settings,** click **Display,** and select **Dark** to switch to **Dark Mode.**
- To make this setting activate at defined times, click **Dark Mode Settings,** switch on '**Turn on As Scheduled**,' then select either Sunset to Sunrise or **Custom Schedule.**
  - ➤ Your device will use your phone time to define sunset and sunrise.
  - ➤ If you select a custom schedule, you will need to choose start and end times.

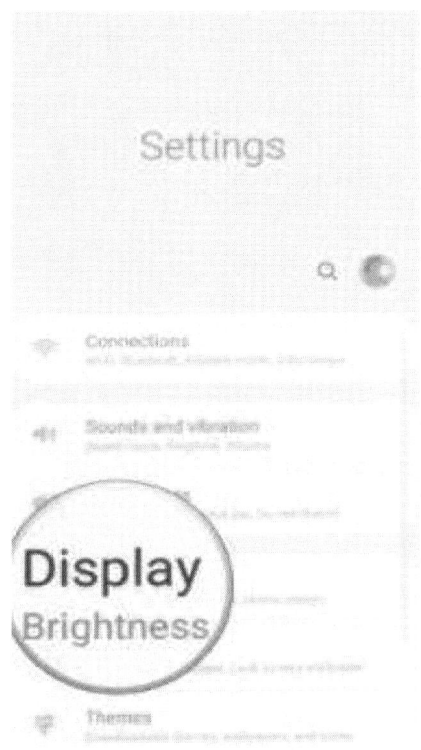 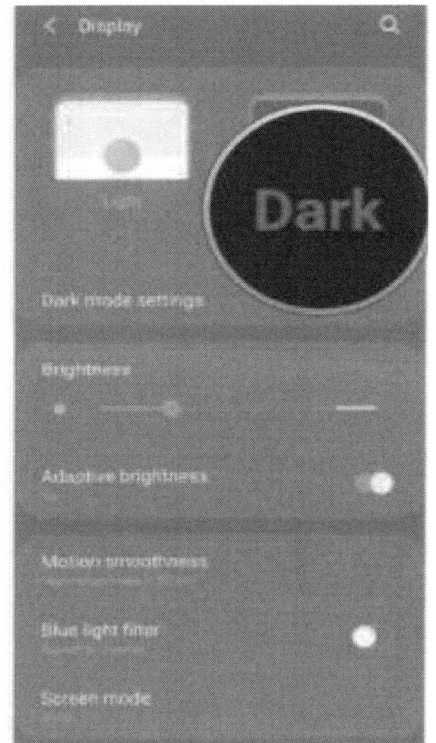

Screen Brightness

Adapt your screen brightness to current lighting conditions

- Open **Settings,** click **Display,** and use the slider under **Brightness** to manually set screen brightness.

- To automatically control the brightness using lighting conditions, turn on the **Adaptive Brightness** switch.

- Another way to adjust screen brightness is to swipe down from the topmost part of your screen and use the slider to set the screen brightness.

Motion Smoothness

By increasing the screen's refresh rate, you will enjoy more realistic animations and smoother scrolling.

- Open **Settings,** click **Display,** and tap **Motion Smoothness.**
- Select an option and click **Apply.**

Eye Comfort Shield

This helps to reduce light strain on the eyes. You can also set up a schedule for this.

- Open **Settings,** click **Display,** and tap **Eye Comfort Shield.**
- Turn on the switch and then choose either **Adaptive** or **Custom.** Use custom to set your own schedule or click **Adaptive** to get the

device to automatically adjust the screen colors using the time of the day.

Screen Mode

These are the different colors that you can use for your screen display.

- Open **Settings,** click **Display,** and tap **Screen Mode.**
- Click on an option to preview and select it.

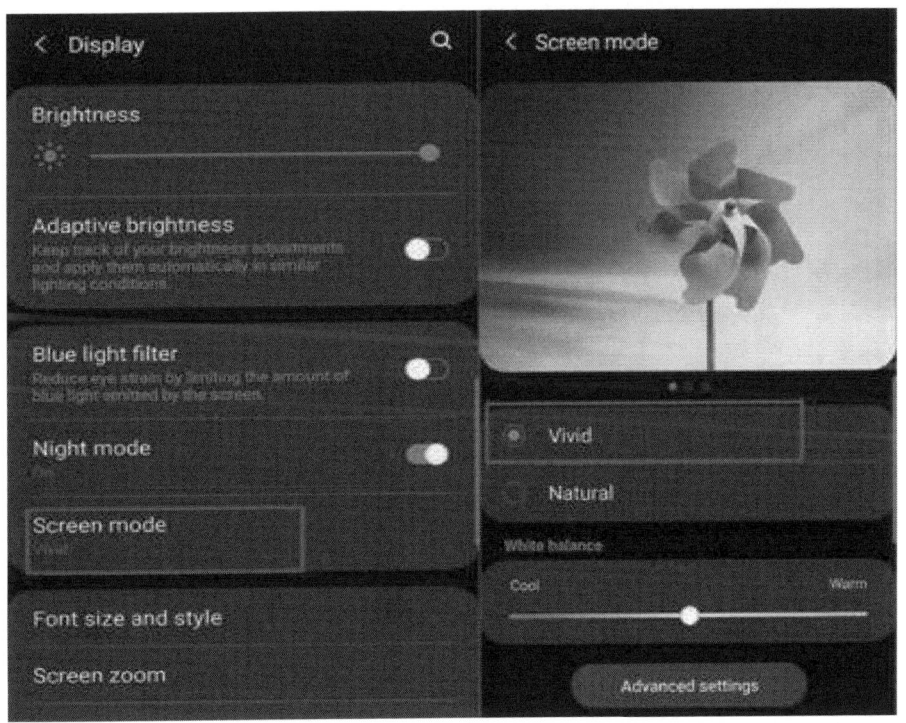

Note that Vivid has more colors than Natural. If you select **Vivid,** you may click **Advanced Settings** to change the intensity of each color.

Screen Resolution

This setting applies to Galaxy S22 Ultra only. You can increase the screen resolution to brighten image quality or reduce it to save your battery level.

- Open **Settings,** click **Display,** and tap **Screen Resolution.**
- Set your desired resolution and press **Apply.**

Note that some apps may close if the resolution is higher or lower than the default.

Font Style and Size

Use any font style and size of your choice.

- Open **Settings,** click **Display,** and tap **Font Size and Style.**
- Click **Font Style** to choose a style or click **Download Fonts** to get new fonts.

- Turn on **Bold Font** to make the fonts look weightier.
- Use the **Font Size** slider to set the text font size.

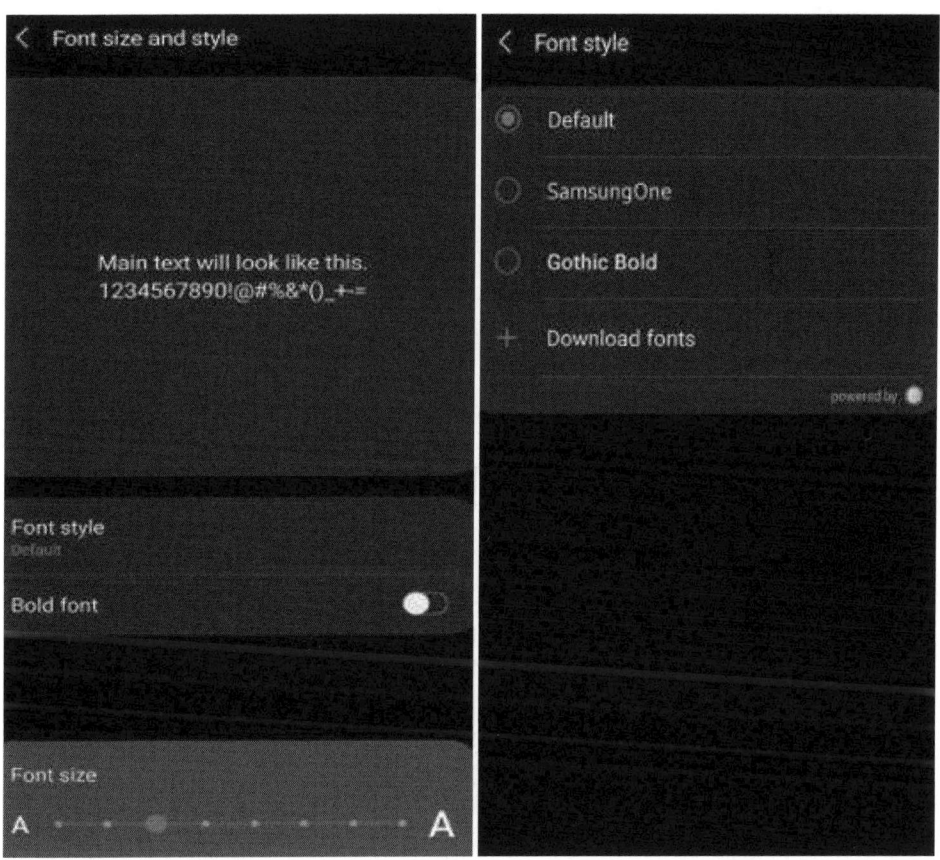

Screen Zoom

Zoom in or out on your screen to make it bigger or smaller

- Open **Settings,** click **Display,** and tap **Screen Zoom.**
- Use the slider to set the screen size of choice.

Full-Screen Apps
Hide the camera cut-out area with a black bar and view select apps in full screen

- Open **Settings,** click **Display,** and tap **Full Screen Apps.**
- Then enable the feature for the apps of your choice.

Screen Timeout
Configure your screen to go to sleep after a defined time of inactivity

- Open **Settings,** click **Display,** and tap **Screen Timeout.**
- Then choose a time of your choice.
- You can also manually press the side button once to put the phone to sleep before the selected time.

Accidental Touch Protection

Prevent your device's screen from detecting and responding to touch input when the phone is in a dark area like a bag or your pocket.

- Open **Settings,** click **Display,** and turn on **Accidental Touch Protection.**

Touch Sensitivity

Configure your phone to respond faster to touches when using screen protectors

- Open **Settings,** click **Display,** and turn on **Touch Sensitivity.**

Screen Saver

Use your photos or select colors to show on your screen while the phone is charging or asleep.

- Open **Settings,** click **Display,** and tap **Screen Saver.**

- Click **Colors** to use different preset colors or click **Photos** and tap ⚙ to choose a picture.

- You may also click **Photo Table** to have different photos in a photo table or select **Photo Frame** to have the pictures in a frame.

  Click ⚙ beside the option to select the photos.

- Select **None** to stop using a screen saver.

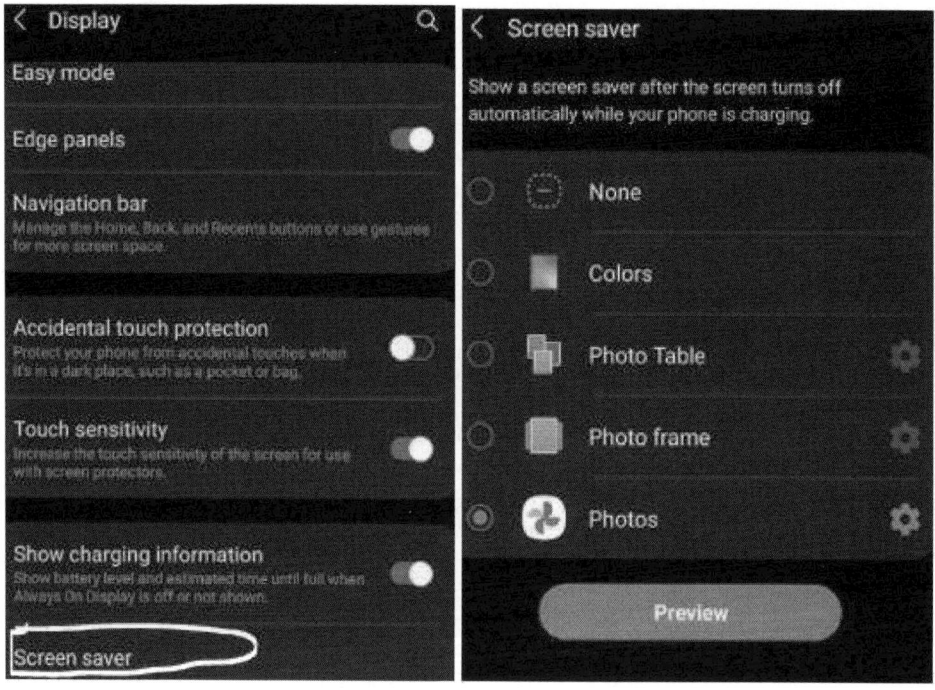

One-Handed Mode
This setting reduces your screen size so that you can operate your phone using one hand.

- Open **Settings**, click **Advanced Features,** and tap **One-Handed Mode.**
- Toggle on the ⬤ switch and select an option: **Gestures** or **Button.**
    - ➤ **Gesture:** to reduce the screen layout, place a finger in the center, close to the bottom of your screen, and swipe down.
    - ➤ **Button:** press the home button twice to reduce the screen layout.
- Press the screen again to return to the full screen.

Chapter 28: Lock Screen and Security

You can secure your smartphone by choosing a lock screen security method like PIN, password, pattern, or swipe. Press the side key once to lock your screen. Press the same key once/ double-tap the screen to turn it, and then swipe up or left to unlock the screen (enter the password or PIN (if required))

Set a Secure Screen Lock

Samsung considers the password, PIN, or pattern as its most secure screen lock. To choose a lock method,

- Open **Settings** and click **Lock Screen.**
- Select **Screen Lock Type,** choose an option.
- Turn on the ⬭ switch to allow notifications to show on the lock screen. You will see the following options:
    - ➢ **Details:** show information about the notification on the lock screen

- ➢ **Icon:** show only the app icons without any details
- ➢ **Transparency:** set how obvious you want the notification cards to be.
- ➢ **Hide Content:** totally disable notifications.
- ➢ **Auto-reverse Text Color:** change the color of the notification text to match the background color.
- ➢ **Notifications to Show:** select the notifications you want to see on the lock screen
- ➢ **Show on Always on Display:** allow notifications when Always on Display is turned on.

- Select **Done** to save and exit.
- Then turn on **Always on Display** to have the Always on Display even on the locked screen.

Change Lock Screen Method

- Go to the Settings app and click **Lock Screen.**

- Click **Screen Lock Type** to set a PIN, Password, or other methods for the lock screen. Choose a PIN or password to protect your device.

Factory Data Reset for Lock Screen

One setting you can do on this screen is to set up your phone to automatically carry out a factory data reset should you enter the wrong unlock code multiple times.

- Go to the Settings app and click **Lock Screen.**

- Click **Secure Lock Settings** and enter your PIN or Password.

- Then switch on the **Auto Factory Reset** button to turn on the option.

Smart Lock

This setting automatically unlocks your phone once it detects that you are in trusted locations or around other trusted devices. You need to have a screen lock to use this feature.

- Open **Settings** and click **Lock Screen.**
- Click **Smart Lock,** enter your lock details, then click each option on the next page and turn on the ⬤ switch or add devices.

Screen Lock Settings

Configure the settings for your security lock. You must select a secure screen lock to use this feature.

- Open **Settings** and click **Lock Screen.**
- Click **Screen Lock Setting,** enter your lock details, and then turn on any desired settings:
    - ➢ Click **Auto Lock When Screen Turns Off** and choose when your phone should be locked after the screen goes off.

- Turn on **Lock Instantly with Side Key** to lock the device by pressing the side key once.
- Turn on **Auto Factory Reset** to configure the phone to return to its default settings and erase all data once the wrong secure lock is entered 15 times.
- Turn on **Lock Network and Security** if you want to block turning off mobile data and Wi-Fi from the locked screen
- Turn on **Show Lockdown Option** to see a power button option that disables biometric unlock, smart lock, and notifications on the lock screen.

Chapter 29: Always on Display

With Always on Display (AOD), you do not need to unlock your screen to see your missed notifications, check the date and time and view other information.

Turn on Always on Display
- Open **Settings** and click **Lock Screen.**
- Select **Always on Display** and turn on the ⬤ switch.
- Then select when to see notifications and the clock on your locked screen.

Show Music Information on AOD
See the music control button on the AOD screen.

- Open **Settings** and click **Lock Screen.**
- Select **Always on Display** and turn on the ⬤ switch.
- Then turn on the **Show Music Information** ⬤ switch

AOD Clock Style

Change the style of the clock in the Always on Display

- Open **Settings** and click **Lock Screen.**
- Select **Always on Display** and turn on the ⬤ switch.
- Click **Clock Style,** then select a design and use the color palette at the bottom to choose a color.
- Click **Done** to finish.

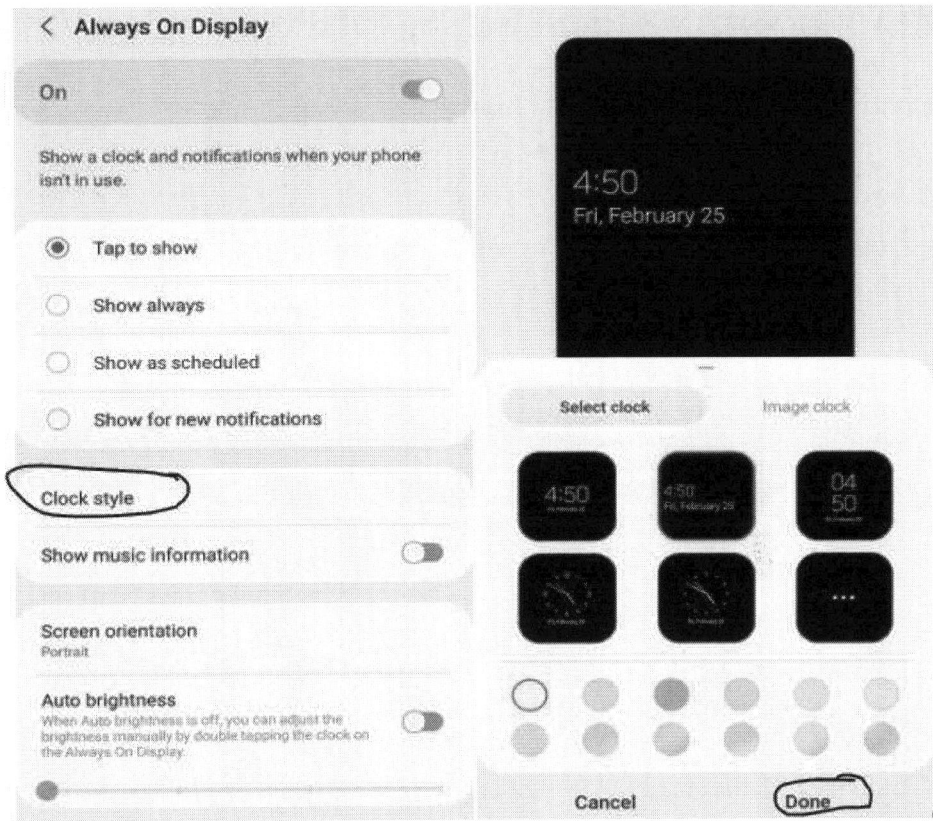

AOD Auto-Brightness

Turn on this feature to adjust the brightness of the AOD screen with the lighting in your environment.

- Open **Settings** and click **Lock Screen**.
- Select **Always on Display** and turn on the ⬤ switch.
- Then turn on the **Auto Brightness** ⬤ switch

- Or use the slider under to set the brightness level.

AOD Themes
Chose a customized theme for the AOD screen

- Tap and hold any empty space on the home screen until you see the settings option.
- Press **Themes** and select **AODs.**
- Click an AOD theme to download it.
- Then tap ≡, click **My Stuff,** and select **AODs** to see the themes you downloaded.
- Now click an AOD theme and press **Apply.**

Chapter 30: Mobile Continuity

Link your device to your computers and other mobile devices and access your storage and other features.

Link to Window

Connect the S22 to your Windows computer and access your phone content on the computer.

- Open **Settings** and click **Advanced Features.**
- Click **Link to Windows** and use the prompts to connect your phone to your computer.

Once connected, you can perform the following actions:

- Move pictures from your phone to your laptop. Open and edit the images on your computer. Share photos with your phone contacts.
- See a pop-up message window on your PC when you have a new message.
- Manage notifications from your computer

- Live stream the S22 screen on your computer.
- Use your computer mouse and keyboard to operate your phone. And lots more.

Samsung DeX

Connect your phone to your TV or PC for great multitasking activity. Operate the phone right on the TV or use the phone as a trackpad for the tv or PC. You would need to download Samsung DeX on the TV and PC to use this feature. To turn on,

- Open **Settings** and click **Advanced Features.**
- Click **Samsung DeX** and turn on the switch.
- You will see instructions to guide you through the connection process.

Continue Apps on Other Devices

Once you sign in on all your Galaxy devices using the same Samsung account details, you can start an action in one device and complete it in another.

- Open **Settings** and click **Advanced Features.**
- Click **Continue Apps on Other Devices** and turn on the ⬤ switch.
- The connection will take effect automatically across all linked devices.

Multi-Window
Use different apps simultaneously by splitting the apps on the screen.

- Tap |||, click the first app you want to use, and select **Open in Split Screen View.**
- The first app will open at the top of your screen. Click the other half of the screen to open a new app.
- Use the line in the middle to increase or reduce the screen space for either of the apps.

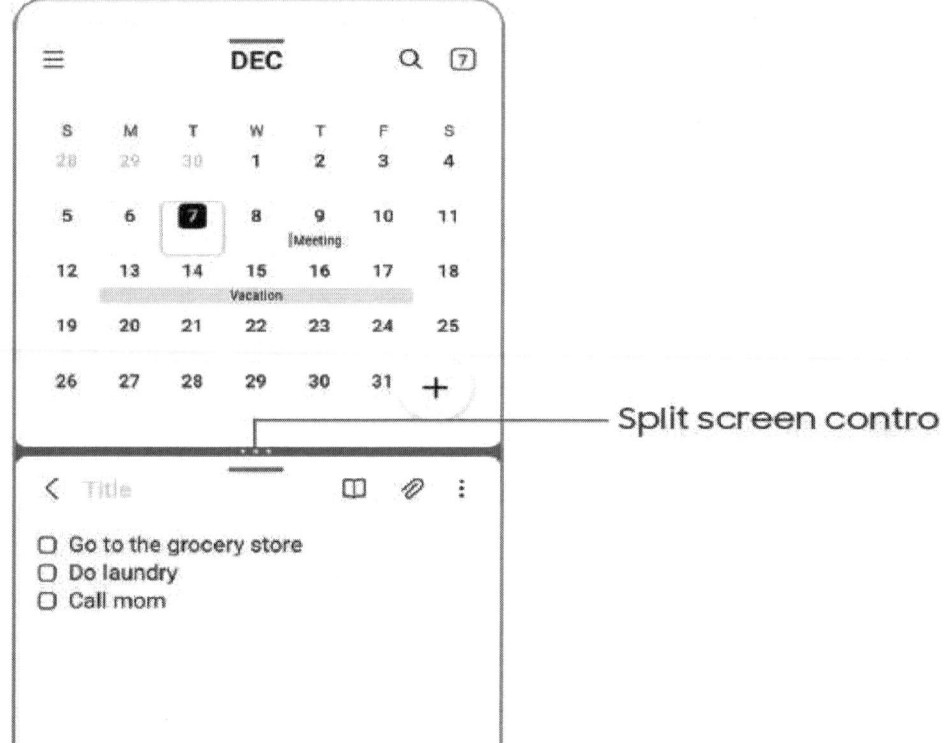

Split screen contro

Window Controls

This customizes the appearance of app windows in the split-screen

- Press the center of the line in the middle for the following:

- Tap ⇅ to switch the placement of both apps.

- Press ⊞ to add the app combination to the edge panel.

Chapter 31: Location Services

This service combines mobile network, GPS, and Wi-fi to tell your device's current location. You need to turn on the location service to use Find My Mobile.

Turn on Location Services
- Open **Settings** and click **Location.**
- Then turn on the ⬤switch.

App Permissions
See apps that have access to your device location and change permission for such apps.

- Open **Settings,** click **Location,** and select **App Permissions.** To configure permission for an app, click the app and choose one location access option.

Recent Access
See the apps that recently accessed your location

- Open **Settings,** click **Location,** and turn on the ⬤switch.
- You will see the list under **Recent Access.**

Emergency Location Service

For regions where this service is available, your smartphone can automatically share your location with the emergency response team after you text or call the emergency number. To turn on,

- Open **Settings** and select **Safety and Emergency.**
- Click **Emergency Location Service** and turn on the ⬤switch.

Chapter 32: Device Maintenance

Quick Optimization

This feature aims to improve your device performance in different ways. It clears unneeded content from your phone storage, shows apps that consume excess battery power, closes background apps, scans for malware, and deletes unused files. To use this feature,

- Open **Settings**, click **Battery and device care,** and select **Optimize Now.**

Set Up Quick Charging

Turn on this feature to charge your smartphone quickly:

- Go to the Settings app and click **Battery and Device Care.**
- Choose **Battery,** then click **More Battery Settings**.
- Then choose one of the options below:

> **Super-Fast Charging:** you would need a USB Power Delivery (USD PD) charger to use this option

> **Fast Charging:** you need a charger that supports "Adaptive Fast Charging" for this option.

> **Fast Wireless Charging:** you need a charger that supports "Fast Wireless Charging" for this option.

Tip: turn off the screen or the device to charge the device quickly.

Set Power Sharing Limit
You can customize the S22 to pause power-sharing once the device's battery power goes below a defined level. To do this,

- Go to the Settings app and click **Battery and Device Care.**
- Choose **Battery,** then click **Wireless Power Sharing**.

- Then click **Battery Limit** to choose a limit.

Tips to Save Battery Power

If your battery runs low while you are out, here are a couple of things you can do to conserve your device's battery power:

- Turn off Bluetooth when not in use
- Close apps not in use
- Turn on the power-saving mode
- Put your device to sleep when not in use
- Turn off auto-synching of apps
- Reduce the brightness of the screen
- Reduce the backlight time

View Battery Usage Since Last Full Charge

See how your battery power was used after the last charge.

- Open **Settings**, click **Battery and Device Care**.
- Click **Battery** and click **Usage Since Last Full Charge** for a detailed breakdown.

Battery Power Saving

Limit location checking, app syncing, and background network usage to save battery life.

- Open **Settings**, click **Battery and Device Care**.
- Click **Battery** and turn on **Power Saving.**

Battery Background Usage Limit

See a list of apps you do not use frequently and reduce their battery consumption.

- Open **Settings**, click **Battery and Device Care**.
- Click **Battery,** click **Background Usage Limits,** then turn on **Put Unused Apps to Sleep** .

Adaptive Battery

Reduce the battery consumption of apps you do not use frequently.

- Open **Settings**, click **Battery and Device Care**.

- Click **Battery**, tap **More Battery Settings,** and turn on **Adaptive Battery** ⬤.

Protect Battery
Samsung recommends limiting the maximum battery charge to 85% as this will increase the battery's lifespan. You can configure your phone to stop charging once it gets to 85%

- Open **Settings**, click **Battery and Device Care**.
- Click **Battery**, tap **More Battery Settings,** and turn on **Protect Battery** ⬤.

Manage Storage
See available storage and get a detailed breakdown of how storage is used.

- Open **Settings**, click **Battery and Device Care**.
- Click **Storage** to see usage breakdown. Click a category to see and manage its content

Manage Memory

See how much memory you have left. Having more memory helps to increase your device speed.

- Open **Settings** and click **Battery and Device Care**.
- Click **Memory** to view available memory and tap **Clean Now** to make more space available.
- Click **View More** to know the apps using up memory.
- Tap **Apps not used recently** to see apps in this bracket, then tap ✓ to select or unselect them from the check
- Click **Excluded Apps** to see all the apps exempted from the memory check. Tap + to add or remove apps.

Advanced Device Care Options
For more settings, see below:

- Open **Settings** and click **Battery and Device Care**.

- Tap 🔍 to search for installed or ready to install panels

- Tap 📊 for temperature tips, charging tips, and restart history.

Chapter 33: Troubleshooting

Reset services on your phone, check for software updates, and handle glitches.

System/ Software Updates

Search for new updates and install them on your device.

- Open **Settings** and click **Software Update/ System.**
- Click **Check for Updates** to search for available system updates.
- Click **Check for Software Updates** to search for available software updates.
- Click **Continue Update** to resume a paused update.
- Click **Show Software Update History** for a list of past software updates.
- Click **Smart Updates** to configure the system to automatically install new security updates

Reset all Phone Settings

Delete every setting change and return your phone to its factory default setting. This step will not affect your personal data.

- Open **Settings,** click **General Management,** and click **Reset.**
- Click **Reset All Settings,** select **Reset Settings** and confirm.

Reset Network Setting

Reset every network-related setting, including Bluetooth, mobile data, and Wi-Fi.

- Open **Settings,** click **General Management,** and click **Reset.**
- Click **Reset Network Settings,** select **Reset Settings,** and confirm.

Reset Accessibility Settings

Reset changes made to accessibility settings. This will not affect personal data and downloaded apps.

- Open **Settings,** click **General Management,** and click **Reset.**
- Click **Reset Accessibility Settings,** select **Reset Settings,** and confirm.

Auto-Restart Device

One way to optimize your device is to configure it to restart on its own at a defined time.

- Open **Settings,** click **General Management,** and click **Reset.**
- Click **Auto Restart at Set Times,** turn on the ⬤ switch and set the day and time.

Factory Data Reset

This setting will wipe all data off your device and return it to the state it was in before you turned it on for the first time.

- Open **Settings,** click **General Management,** and click **Reset.**
- Click **Factory Data Reset,** select **Reset,** and the screen will guide you on the next steps.

Remove Secure Lock Screen

To stop using a secure lock screen,

- Open **Settings** and click **Lock Screen.**
- Tap **Screen Lock Type** and choose **None** or **Swipe.**

Chapter 34: Digital Wellbeing and Parental Controls

Get a view of the amount of time you spend on your device as well as the apps you use frequently to help you manage your digital habits.

View Dashboard

See a breakdown of your phone usage and activities.

- Open **Settings** and click **Digital Wellbeing and Parental Controls.**
- Then click the top part of the screen that shows the hour to see screen time, notification received from apps, and the number of times you unlocked your device.

Set Screen Time Goal

Set the number of hours you want to be on your phone daily.

- Open **Settings** and click **Digital Wellbeing and Parental Controls.**
- Click **Screen Time** and tap **Set Goal**.

- Choose the time and press **Done.**

App Timers

Set the number of hours you want to spend on an app daily.

- Open **Settings** and click **Digital Wellbeing and Parental Controls.**
- Click **App Timers,** click each app, set the time, and press **Done.**

Focus Mode

Focus mode stops you from using apps within the active period to avoid distraction.

- Open **Settings** and click **Digital Wellbeing and Parental Controls.**
- Click **Focus Mode,** select **Work** or **Me Time,** click **Edit** to select and unselect apps you want to block during this period, then click **Start.** You may also click **Add** to customize the focus mode
- Once you are done, press **End Focus Mode.**

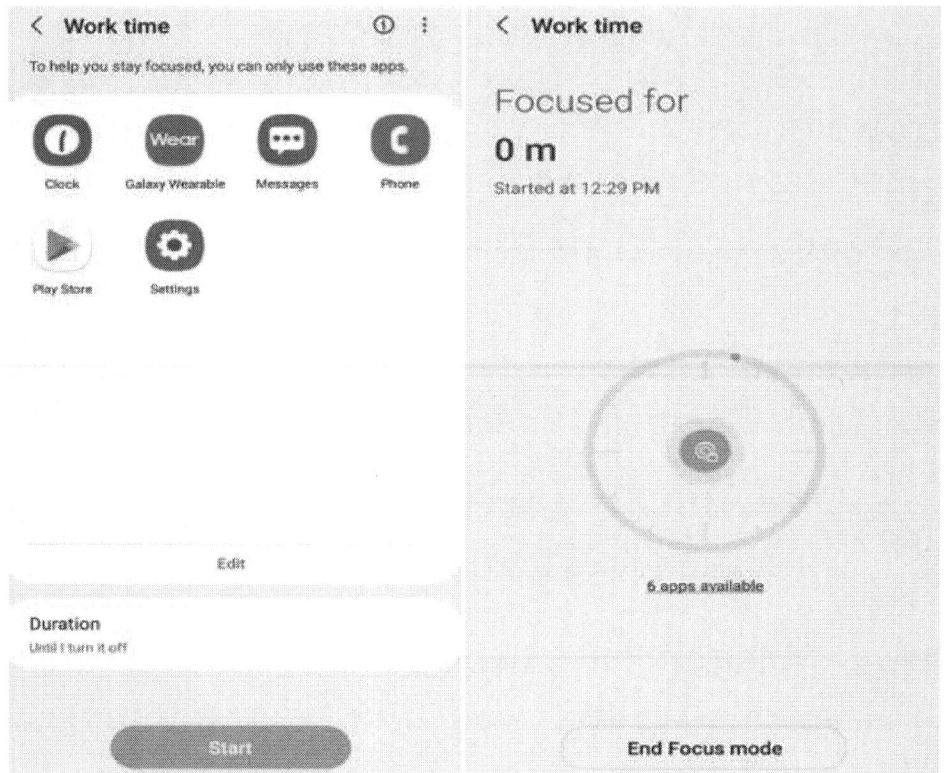

Bedtime Mode

Bedtime mode would turn your screen color to grayscale, and mute alerts, calls, and all sounds

- Open **Settings** and click **Digital Wellbeing and Parental Controls.**
- Click **Bedtime Mode** and press **Start.**
- Press **Turn on Now** to use the feature immediately, press **End Bedtime Mode** to turn off.

- You may also set it as a schedule. Switch on **Turn on As Scheduled** then set the days and time.

Volume Monitor

Periodically check the sound level on your device to protect your ears when using headphones.

- Open **Settings** and click **Digital Wellbeing and Parental Controls.**
- Click **Volume Monitor** and tap ⋮.
- Select **Use Volume Monitor** and turn on the switch.
- The volume data will appear on the Volume Monitor screen.

Driving Monitor

This tells you the app you use the most while your phone is connected to your car's Bluetooth.

- Open **Settings** and click **Digital Wellbeing and Parental Controls.**
- Press **Driving Monitor** and tap **Start.**

- Follow the onscreen prompt to finish.

Parental Control

With Google's Family Link App, you can supervise and monitor your child's online presence. You can select apps and set limits.

- Open **Settings** and click **Digital Wellbeing and Parental Controls.**
- Tap **Parental Control** and select **Get Started.**
- Follow the onscreen prompt to finish.

Chapter 35: Other Settings

Android Auto

Connect your phone to your car and access certain apps and features on the car screen even while your phone is locked. You need to connect your phone to your car using a USB cable

- Open **Settings** and click **Advanced Features.**
- Select **Android Auto** and click **Connect a Car**.
- Plug one part of the USB cable to your phone and the other end to your car.
- Follow the prompts on your phone to finish the process.
- Turn on your car display, choose **Audio Auto,** and use the steps on the screen to complete the steps.

Your phone's Bluetooth will turn on once the phone is connected using USB.

Dual Messenger

Use two accounts for a single app, like using two WhatsApp, Facebook, or Twitter.

- Open **Settings** and click **Advanced Features.**
- Click **Dual Messenger** and turn on beside each app to duplicate it.
- Turn on **Use Separate Contact List** to choose the contacts that can access the second version.

Smart Suggestions

Receive suggestions to perform certain actions like add events to your calendar or reminder to send a message,

- Open **Settings** and click **Advanced Features.**
- Click **Smart Suggestions** and turn on the button.

Medical Info

Third parties, including emergency responders, can view your medical information even with a locked screen. To set this up,

- Open **Settings** and click **Safety and Emergency.**
- Press **Medical Info** and tap ✏ at the top.
- Fill in every necessary information and press **Save.**
- Repeat these steps to delete, change or add.

Quick Share

Others with a Samsung account can share files with your Galaxy S22 using the Quick Share feature.

- Open **Settings** and click **Advanced Features.**
- Click **Samsung Account** to sign in if not signed in yet.
- Click **Phone Name** to use a name that you want others to see.

- Click **Who can Share with You** to select those that should be able to send you files.
- Turn on **Show my Position to Others** so people can know when you are available to receive a file.
- Turn on **Convert Videos to Compatible Format** to change video resolution to standard.
- Click **Link Sharing History** to see all the links others shared with you.
- Turn on **Use Wi-Fi Only** to limit this feature to only when the device is on Wi-Fi connection.
- Click **Auto Delete Expired Files** to choose what to do with the files.
- Click **Privacy Notice** to learn how Samsung manages your information shared through this feature.

Samsung Labs

This setting allows you to test experimental features like opening several apps in split-screen. To turn on,

- Open **Settings** and click **Advanced Features.**
- Click **Labs** and turn on ⬤ any experimental feature

About Phone

See details of your phone, including software and hardware versions, serial number, and more

- Open **Settings** and click **About Phone.**
- You will find different information about the phone, including model name, number, IMEI, and more.
- Click other information tabs to view more.

Conclusion

The Galaxy S22 series is packed with several features that will help to make your work and life easier. I hope you find this user guide helpful in finding and learning about the different things and features you can do with your new device.

Thank you!

Printed in Great Britain
by Amazon